Microsoft Windows Vista
– an Ultimate Guide

Other Titles of Interest from Bernard Babani (publishing) Ltd

BP573 Using Windows Media Player 11

BP579 Upgrading To and Troubleshooting Windows Vista

BP580 Windows Vista for Beginners

BP581 Windows Vista Explained

BP583 Microsoft Office 2007 Explained

BP614 Computing with Vista for the Older Generation

Other Titles by the same author

BP565	Using Microsoft Windows XP Media Center 2005
BP567	How To Set Up Your Home or Small Business Network
BP571	Getting More From Your Microsoft Xbox 360

Microsoft Windows Vista – an Ultimate Guide

by

Andrew Edney

Bernard Babani (publishing) Ltd
The Grampians
Shepherds Bush Road
London W6 7NF
England
www.babanibooks.com

Please Note

Although every care has been taken with the production of this book to ensure that any projects, designs, modifications and/or programs, etc, contained herewith, operate in a correct and safe manner and also that any components specified are normally available in Great Britain, the Publishers and Author(s) do not accept responsibility in any way for the failure (including fault in design) of any project, design, modification or program to work correctly or to cause damage to any equipment that it may be connected to or used in conjunction with, or in respect of any other damage or injury that may be so caused, nor do the Publishers accept responsibility in any way for the failure to obtain specified components.

Notice is also given that if equipment that is still under warranty is modified in any way or used or connected with home-built equipment then that warranty may be void.

ISBN 978 0 85934 578 1

First Published – May 2007

British Library Cataloguing in Publication Data

A catalogue record for this book is available from the British Library

Cover design by Gregor Arthur

Printed and bound in Great Britain by Cox & Wyman Ltd, Reading, Berks

About this Book

Pretty much every household these days has at least one computer in it. Some have more than one.

Most people are currently using Microsoft Windows XP as their operating system, either Home edition or Professional edition. There are also a small number of people who still use very old systems such as Windows 95 and 98 or Windows Millennium.

Windows Vista is the latest in a very long line of desktop operating systems from Microsoft. This time there are a number of different editions to choose from, which each providing something different depending on the user's needs.

Microsoft's goal is for one of these editions to be used wherever you use a computer, for example at home or in the office at work.

This book will look at the different editions of Windows Vista, take a look at some of the new functionality and really go in depth into some of the exciting new features, such as Windows Media Center which is now part of the operating system.

This book is an indispensable companion to anyone who is thinking about upgrading to Windows Vista or who wants to know more about their new operating system, and it applies to all editions of Vista.

Please note that his book is not an authorised edition or supported by Microsoft.

Conventions

Throughout this book, you will see a number of information boxes, bounded with either a double line like this…

DESIGNATING A WARNING

…or indeed, a single line, like this…

DESIGNATING A NOTE, POINT OF INTEREST OR USEFUL TIP

Procedures and walkthroughs are shown as numerical lists, like this:

1. Step 1
2. Step 2

All diagrams and Figures have a two-digit reference number containing the Chapter number, followed by the Figure number within that Chapter. For example, Figure 1-1 represents the first Figure in Chapter 1.

About the Author

Andrew Edney has been an IT consultant for over 12 years and over the course of his career has worked for a range of high-tech companies, such as Microsoft, Hewlett Packard and Fujitsu Services. He has a wide range of experience in virtually all aspects of Microsoft's computing solutions, having designed and architected large enterprise solutions for government and private sector customers. Over the years, Andrew had made a number of guest appearances at major industry events, presenting on a wide range of Information Systems subjects, such as an appearance at the annual Microsoft Exchange Conference in Nice where he addressed the Microsoft technical community on Mobility Computing. Andrew is currently involved in numerous Microsoft beta programmes, including next generation Windows operating systems and next generation Microsoft Office products, and actively participates in all Windows Media Center beta programmes. On top of all of this, Andrew runs his own IT consulting company, Firebird Consulting and has currently authored 7 books.

Andrew lives in Wiltshire with his partner, Katy, and their two cats and can be reached at andrew@firebirdconsulting.co.uk.

Acknowledgements

I would like to offer my thanks to my family and friends for their support and assistance during the long months of writing this book. In addition to the people explicitly named below, I would also like to offer my thanks to all the staff at Babani for publishing my book.

Primarily, thanks must go to Katy for her support and thanks to Apollo and Starbuck for keeping me calm when I got too stressed out.

I would also like to thank Rosie for her help and input.

To anyone I might have missed, a heartfelt thanks goes out to all of you for making this possible. Once again, it's been a pleasure.

For Mum and Dad – thanks for buying me that first computer all those years ago and getting me interested in this stuff. See, I told you it wouldn't be another five minute wonder.

Trademarks

Microsoft, Windows XP and **Windows Vista** are either registered trademarks or trademarks of the Microsoft Corporation.

All other brand names and product names used in this book are recognised as trademarks, or registered trademarks of their respective companies.

Contents

Conventions vi

PART 1 An Introduction to Windows Vista

1. Introduction to Windows Vista 3

Windows Vista Editions 3
Windows Vista Home Basic 5
Windows Vista Home Premium 6
Windows Vista Ultimate 7
Windows Vista Business 8
Windows Vista Enterprise 9
Windows Vista Starter 10
Edition Features Breakdown 10

Summary 12

PART 2 Installing, Upgrading and Setting Up Windows Vista

2. Installation and Setup 15

Hardware Requirements 16
Vista Ultimate, Home Premium, Enterprise and Business 16
Vista Home Basic 17
Vista Starter 17
Additional requirements to use certain features 18
Vista Capable and Vista Premium Ready PCs 18

Upgrading 19
Operating System Upgrade Options 20
Windows Easy Transfer 21
Exporting the Files and Settings 22
Importing the Files and Settings 29
Windows Vista Upgrade Advisor 33

Installing the Windows Vista Upgrade Advisor 34
Running the Windows Vista Upgrade Advisor 36
Performing the Upgrade 42

A Clean Install **48**

Post Installation Tasks **60**

Activating Windows Vista **62**

Windows Anytime Upgrade **65**

PART 3 Getting the Most From Windows Vista

3. The New Desktop 71

The Start Menu **71**

Explorer **73**

Aero **75**
Flip 76
Flip 3D 77

Other Improvements **78**
ClearType 78
Dialog Boxes 79
Wizards 79

Summary **79**

4. Personalisation 81

Windows Experience Index **81**

Windows Sidebar and Gadgets **84**

Summary **87**

5. Useful Tools and Applications 89

Welcome Center **89**

Control Panel **91**

Windows Backup and Restore **93**
Performing a Backup 94
Performing a Restore 100

Summary **105**

6. Networking **107**

Wired **107**

Wireless **108**

Network and Sharing Center **112**
Network Map 113
Customising Network Settings 114

Summary **115**

7. Internet Explorer 7 **117**

Searching the Internet **118**

Tabbed Browsing **120**

Favourites **124**

Security Features **125**
The Pop-Up Blocker 126
Phishing Filter 128
Protected Mode 131

RSS Feeds **132**

Summary **134**

8. Media Player 11 **135**

Configuring Media Player **135**

The New Interface 140

The Library 141

Ripping Music to your Library 143
Changing the Rip Options 145

Playlists 147

Burning Music CDs 148

Sync 150

Media Guide 151

The Mini Player 151

Summary 152

9. Vista Media 153

Windows Movie Maker 153

Windows Photo Gallery 163
Adding Your Pictures to the Gallery 164
Fixing Your Pictures 167
Online Printing 168
Printing Your Pictures Yourself 170
Slide Shows 171

Windows DVD Maker 172

Summary 182

10. Windows Media Center 183

What Does It Do? 184

Requirements 185

Setting Up Media Center 186

The Guide 189

TV and Movies 192

Watching DVDs 193

Music and Radio 195

Pictures and Videos 197

Writing CDs and DVDs 198

Media Center Extenders 199

Online Media 201

Summary 202

11. Security 203

User Account Control 204

Windows Defender 205

The Windows Firewall 208

Security Center 211

Parental Controls 213

Summary 216

12. Troubleshooting 217

Memory Issues 217

Internet Connection Problems 221

Reliability and Performance Monitor 223

Problem Reports and Solutions 226

Summary 227

Index **229**

PART 1
An Introduction to Windows Vista

1

Introduction to Windows Vista

Thank you for buying this book. Hopefully by the time you have finished going through it you will have a better understanding of what Windows Vista is, which version is right for you and what it can do to make your life easier.

Vista is the latest in a long line of operating systems from Microsoft and according to Microsoft is the easiest, safest and most entertaining operating system yet.

In this chapter, you will learn about the different editions of Windows Vista and what they contain.

Windows Vista Editions

There are actually six different editions of Windows Vista, although not all of them are available to everyone as you will soon see. Choosing the best edition for your needs is very important. Whilst the easiest option may be to buy Vista

Ultimate because it has everything, it is also the most expensive, and as such you may not want to pay that much for your operating system.

Microsoft have three main groups in mind when it comes to the different editions of Vista – home users (or consumers), small business users and medium and large organisations.

Previously with Windows XP, there were special editions released, namely Windows XP Media Center edition and also a Windows XP Tablet edition. With the release of Windows Vista, those special editions have now become part of Vista and are no longer separate editions.

> It is important to note that not all editions of Windows Vista provide certain functionality – more of this later.

For those users who have hardware that supports 64-bit computing, Windows Vista provides built-in support with all versions except the Starter edition.

> All versions of Windows Vista are on the installation DVD, including the 32-bit and 64-bit editions – when you enter your product key the edition that is associated with that key is installed.

Windows Vista Home Basic

Windows Vista Home Basic is the basic option for the home (consumer) user. It contains everything you need to get up and running with Vista, and includes:

- Windows Photo Gallery
- Internet Explorer 7
- Windows Defender

Figure 1-1 Windows Vista Home Basic

It is the cheapest of the all the editions, but its built-in functionality is limited.

Windows Vista Home Premium

The next edition up from Home Basic is Windows Vista Home Premium. It contains everything from Home Basic, and in addition some of the highlights include:

- Windows Media Center
- Windows Aero
- Windows DVD Maker
- Tablet PC functionality

Figure 1-2 Windows Vista Home Premium

For most home users, Vista Home Premium is likely to be the edition of choice. It doesn't come with everything, but for most people it will have everything they need.

As mentioned, it comes preinstalled with Windows Media Center so if you have Vista Premium installed you can start enjoying a whole new media watching experience.

For more on Windows Media Center, take a look at Chapter 10.

Windows Vista Ultimate

If you want the best of the best, and you want it all in one package, then Vista Ultimate is the edition for you.

Figure 1-3 Windows Vista Ultimate

This is the edition that Microsoft recommends for the home user and the small business user who wants it all.

Windows Vista Business

If you want an edition for use in your business, or on your laptop, then you should consider Vista Business. It contains most of the features of Vista Home Basic, with the exception of some of the entertainment features. In addition to those features, Vista Business also contains:

- Windows Aero
- Tablet PC functionality
- Networking features such as Group Policy support
- Fax and Scan facilities

Figure 1-4 Windows Vista Business

Windows Vista Enterprise

This edition of Windows Vista is only available to those people with a Microsoft Software Assurance agreement.

It contains all of the features of Vista Business, but also includes:

- Windows BitLocker Drive Encryption
- Licensing rights to four virtual operating systems
- Subsystem for UNIX-based Applications (SUA)

Windows Vista Starter

This is the last edition that is available, and it is only available in countries that have been categorised as "emerging", so if you are in a country such as the United Kingdom or the United States, then you will not be able to buy this edition.

For the remainder of the book, only the four main editions (Home Basic, Home Premium, Business and Ultimate) will be covered.

Edition Features Breakdown

By far the easiest way to compare the different editions of Vista and what they contain is to look on the Microsoft website and look for the feature you are interested in and check which edition or editions it comes with. Table 1-1 replicates some of that information for you.

Table 1-1 is by no means the complete list of features so if you are not sure, or the feature you are interested in is not shown, check out the Microsoft website.

Features	Home Basic	Home Premium	Business	Ultimate
Windows Defender and Windows Firewall	√	√	√	√
Instant Search	√	√	√	√
Windows Aero		√	√	√
Tablet PC Support		√	√	√
Windows Media Center		√		√
Movie & DVD Maker		√		√
BitLocker Drive Encryption				√
Networking Center			√	√

Table 1-1 Windows Vista Editions Comparison

Summary

So now you know more about the different editions of Windows Vista and what they contain. In the next chapter you will learn all about installing or upgrading to Windows Vista.

PART 2

Installing, Upgrading and Setting Up Windows Vista

2

Installation and Setup

If you have purchased a computer that comes preinstalled with a version of Windows Vista, you can safely skip this chapter and move on to the next one.

In this chapter you will learn about the recommended hardware requirements for the different editions of Windows Vista. You will also be guided through the process of either upgrading an existing supported operating system, such as Windows XP, to Windows Vista and also performing a clean installation of Windows Vista. You will also see how you can use the File Transfer Wizard to help you to migrate your files and settings from your existing computer to your new Vista computer or installation.

Hardware Requirements

The following are the recommended hardware requirements for the various editions of Windows Vista.

> Remember even though these are the recommended hardware requirements, the better the hardware, the more enjoyable the experience.

Vista Ultimate, Home Premium, Enterprise and Business

- 1 GHz, 32-bit (x86) or 64-bit (x64) processor
- 1 GB of system memory
- 40 GB hard drive with at least 15 GB of available space
- Support for DirectX 9 graphics with:
  - WDDM Driver
  - 128 MB of graphics memory (minimum)
  - Pixel Shader 2.0 in hardware
  - 32 bits per pixel
- DVD-ROM drive
- Audio output

- Internet access

Vista Home Basic

- 1 GHz, 32-bit (x86) or 64-bit (x64) processor
- 512 MB of system memory
- 20 GB hard drive with at least 15 GB of available space
- Support for DirectX 9 graphics and 32 MB of graphics memory
- DVD-ROM drive
- Audio output
- Internet access

Vista Starter

- 800 MHz processor
- 512 MB of system memory
- 20 GB hard drive with at least 15 GB of available space
- Support for Super VGA graphics
- CD-ROM drive

Additional requirements to use certain features

- TV tuner card required for TV functionality supported in Windows Media Center
- Windows Tablet and Touch Technology requires a Tablet PC or a touch screen
- Windows BitLocker Drive Encryption requires a USB flash drive

Vista Capable and Vista Premium Ready PCs

There are also two definitions of PCs – Windows Vista Capable and Windows Vista Premium Ready.

A Windows Vista Capable PC can deliver the core experience of Windows Vista and comes with at a minimum:

- A modern processor (at least 800 MHz)
- 512 MB of system memory
- A graphics processor that is DirectX 9 capable

A Windows Vista Premium Ready PC can run any version of Windows Vista and comes with at a minimum:

- 1 GHz, 32-bit (x86) or 64-bit (x64) processor
- 1 GB of system memory
- A graphics process that runs Windows Aero
- 128 MB of graphics memory
- 20 GB hard drive with at least 15 GB of available space
- DVD-ROM drive
- Audio output
- Internet access

Upgrading

If you want to upgrade your existing computer, there are two different methods for doing it that are available to you. One is the clean install method which effectively installs a clean copy of the chosen edition of Windows Vista on your computer. You then have to reinstall your applications and copy your data back to your computer (assuming you backed up your data before starting the clean install).

The other is known as the upgrade-in-place method. This installs your chosen edition of Windows Vista on top of your existing operating system and enables you to keep your data and as many of your installed applications, that are compatible, as possible.

Operating System Upgrade Options

Table 2-1 shows the supported operating systems and their upgrade options.

	Home Basic	Home Premium	Business	Ultimate
Windows XP Professional	Clean Install	Clean Install	Upgrade-in-place	Upgrade-in-place
Windows XP Home	Upgrade-in-place	Upgrade-in-place	Upgrade-in-place	Upgrade-in-place
Windows XP Media Center	Clean Install	Upgrade-in-place	Clean Install	Upgrade-in-place
Windows XP Tablet PC	Clean Install	Clean Install	Clean Install	Upgrade-in-place
Windows XP Professional x64	Clean Install	Clean Install	Upgrade-in-place	Upgrade-in-place
Windows 2000	Clean Install	Clean Install	Clean Install	Clean Install

Table 2-1 Operating System Upgrade Options

Windows Easy Transfer

Microsoft provide an application to help the backup and restoration of your data if you are using the clean install method. This application is called Windows Easy Transfer and is used to transfer a number of different files and settings from computers running Windows 2000, Windows XP and even Windows Vista.

The types of files and settings include:

- User Accounts
- Files and folders
- Email messages, settings, and contacts
- Photos, music, and videos
- Windows settings
- Program data files and settings
- Internet settings

You can buy the Easy Transfer Cable, as shown in Figure 2-1, from your local computer shop which contains a special USB cable for connecting your old computer to your new computer, if you are planning on building or buying a new one. It also comes with all the software you need to perform the transfer.

Figure 2-1 A Windows Easy Transfer Cable

Exporting the Files and Settings

Another option is to download Windows Easy Transfer for XP (if you are using Windows XP) and use that to backup your software. Windows Vista already has a version of Windows Easy Transfer installed so you don't need to worry about getting software for your Vista installation.

1. Download Windows Easy Transfer for XP from: http://www.microsoft.com:80/downloads/details.aspx?FamilyId=2B6F1631-973A-45C7-A4EC-4928FA173266&displaylang=en.
2. Double-click the file you just downloaded and choose Run when prompted.
3. Follow the steps to install the software on your computer.
4. Launch the software by clicking on Windows Easy Transfer from the Start menu. This will display the Welcome screen as shown in Figure 2-2.

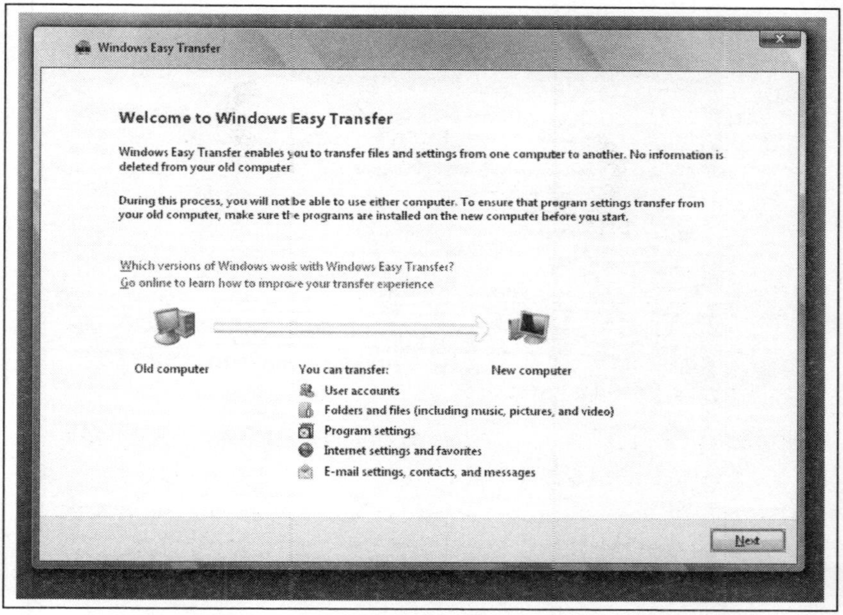

Figure 2-2 The Windows Easy Transfer Welcome Screen

5. Click Next (you may be asked to close any programs that are currently running and may conflict with the transfer process).

6. You are then presented with three options for how you want to transfer the files and settings (as shown in Figure 2-3):

    - Use an Easy Transfer Cable
    - Transfer directly, using a network connection

- Use a CD, DVD, or other removable media

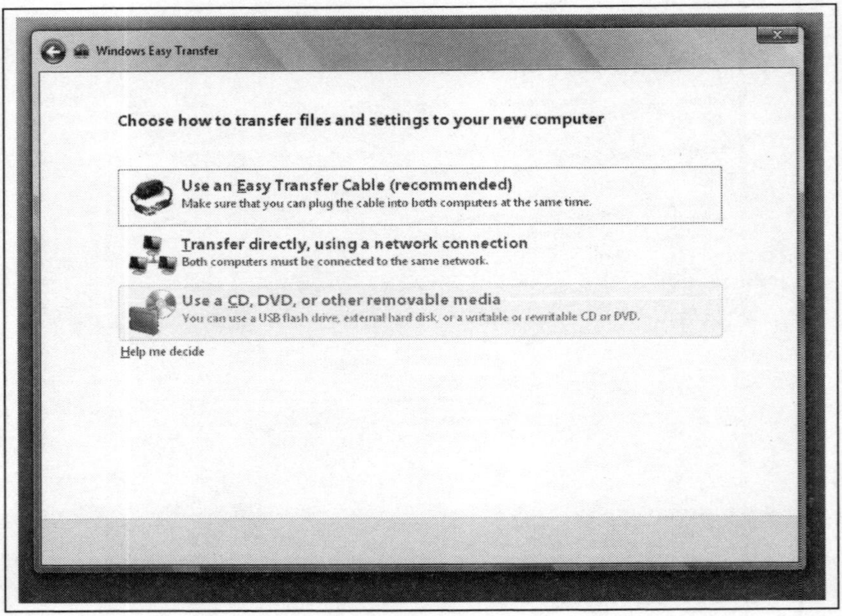

Figure 2-3 Windows Easy Transfer Options

For this example, I am going to select Use a CD, DVD, or other removable media.

7. You are then presented with a further three options for how to transfer the files and settings (as shown in Figure 2-4). They are:
    - CD
    - USB flash drive

- External hard disk or to a network location

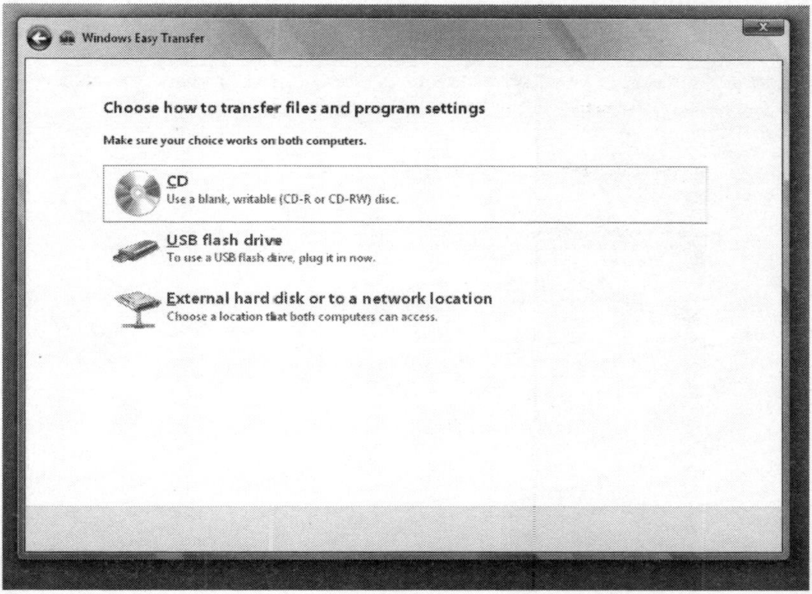

Figure 2-4 Choosing how to transfer the files and settings

For this example, I am going to select USB flash drive, but the process is similar if you select one of the other options.

Whichever method you are planning to use, ensure you have enough free space to successfully perform the transfer.

---

8. Confirm the location of your USB drive and create and confirm a password, if you want to use one (as shown in Figure 2-5). Click Next to continue.

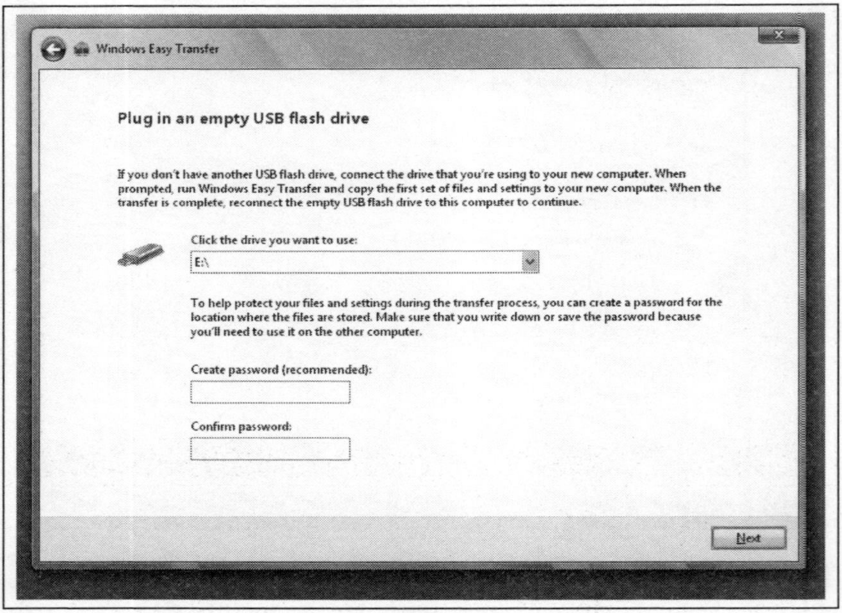

Figure 2-5 Confirming the location of the USB drive and creating a password

9. Choose what you want to transfer from the three options (as shown in Figure 2-6). They are:

   - All user accounts, files, and settings
   - My user account, files, and settings only
   - Advanced options

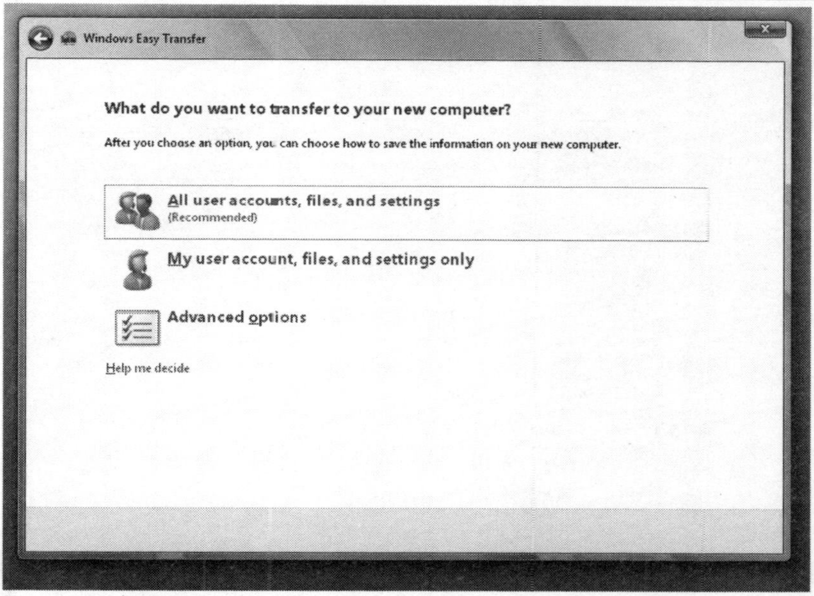

Figure 2-6 Choosing what you want to transfer

The recommended setting is the All user accounts, files, and settings option. However, if you want to specify exactly what you want to transfer you can click on Advanced options and make changes, as shown in Figure 2-7. If you do make changes, click on Next to continue.

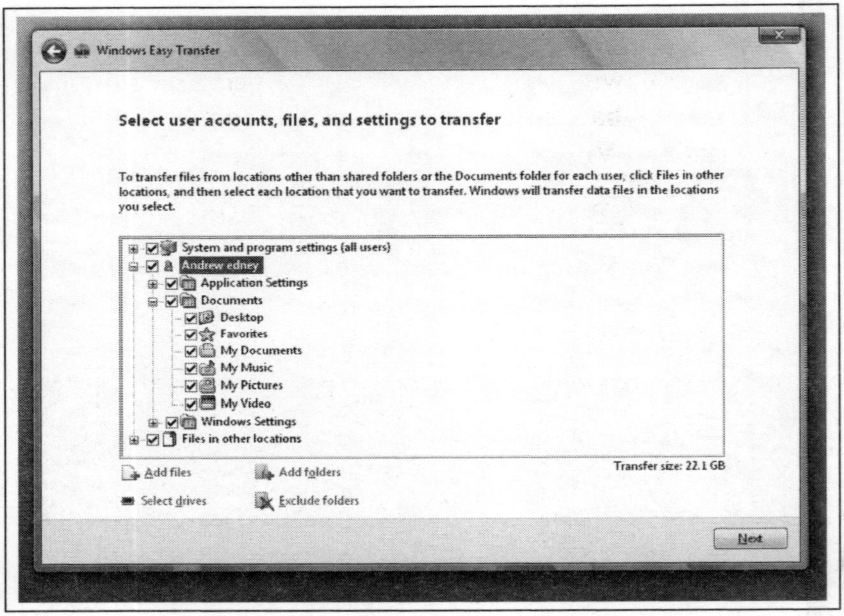

Figure 2-7 Fine tuning your transfer selections

10. Review the selected files and settings and if you are happy with the selection click Transfer, otherwise click back to make changes or click Customize to fine tune the selections.

Depending on how much you are transferring, the process can take some time.

---

11. When the transfer is complete, remove the USB drive, click Close.

Importing the Files and Settings

The following steps should only be performed once you have installed your selected edition of Windows Vista.

1. Put the USB drive into the Windows Vista computer.
2. From the Welcome Center, click on Transfer files and settings, as shown in Figure 2-8. Then click on Start Windows Easy Transfer.

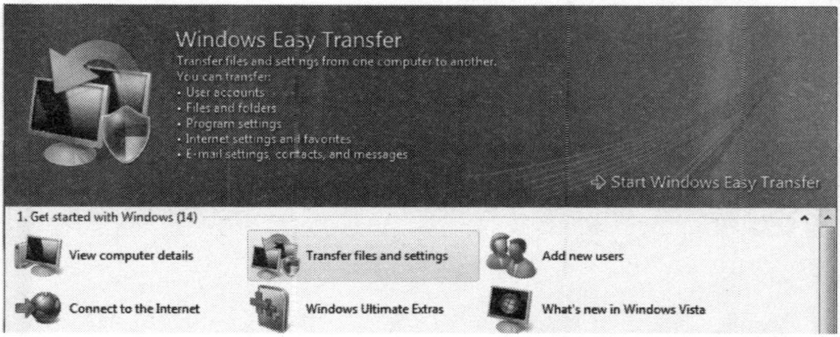

Figure 2-8 Selecting Transfer files and settings from the Welcome Center

3. Click Next (you may be asked to close any programs that are currently running and may conflict with the transfer process).
4. Click on Continue a Transfer in Progress.
5. You will be asked if your computers are connected to a network. If you used a USB device to transfer the files

and settings select No, I've copied files and settings to a CD, DVD, or other removable media.

6. Select where you saved the files and settings, in this case choose On a USB flash drive.
7. Select the location of the USB drive and enter the password if you set one, as shown in Figure 2-9. Click Next to continue.

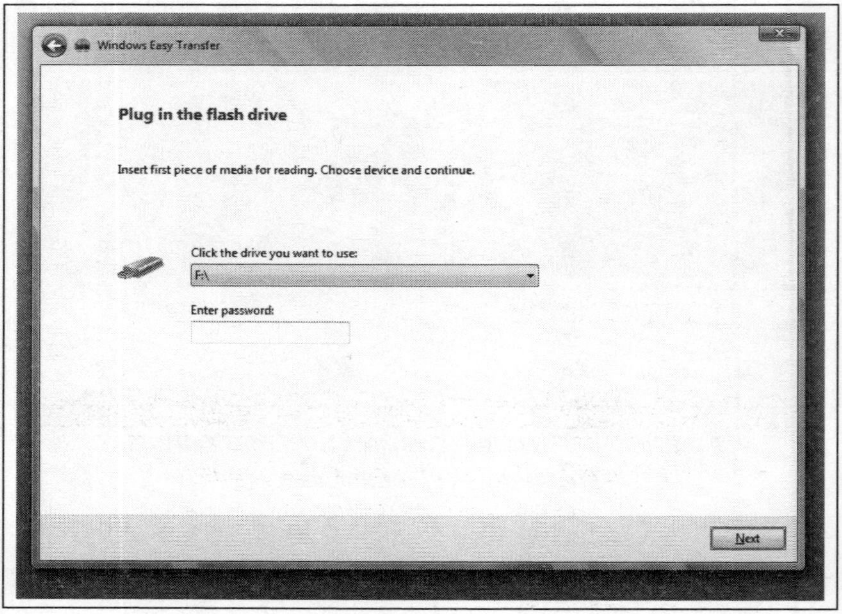

Figure 2-9 Selecting the location of the USB drive

8. Enter a new account name to copy the settings to, or select an existing account name from the drop-down list, as shown in Figure 2-10, then click Next.

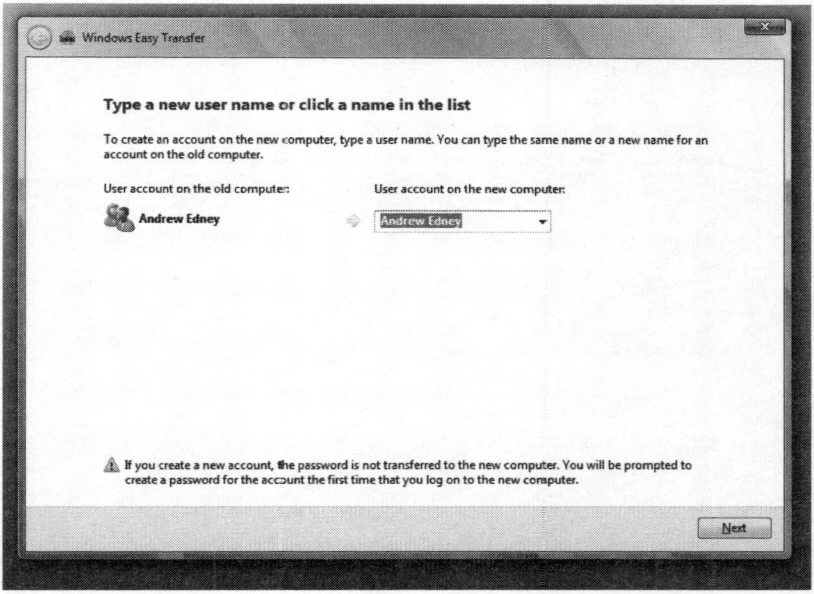

Figure 2-10 Creating a new account or choosing an existing one

---

If you create a new account, the password is not transferred to the new computer.

---

9. Review the selected files and settings, and click Transfer to begin the transfer process.

10. When the transfer is complete, you will be presented with a summary, as shown in Figure 2-11. If you are happy with the results click Close.

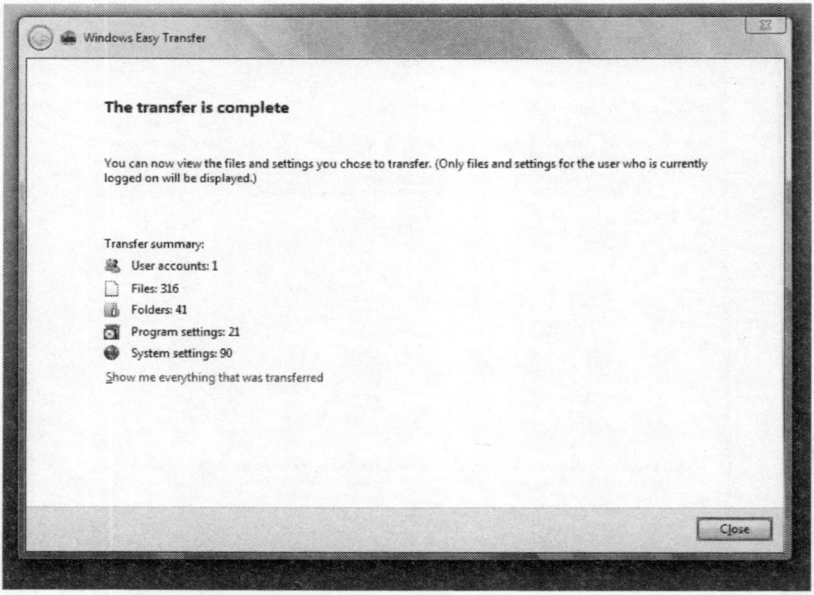

Figure 2-11 Transfer Summary

11. You will need to restart the computer for the changes to take effect.

12. After Windows Vista has restarted, you may be presented with a Protected Content Migration screen, as shown in Figure 2-12. If you are, you will need to enter the password for the "old" account and then click

Confirm my account information and update content protection.

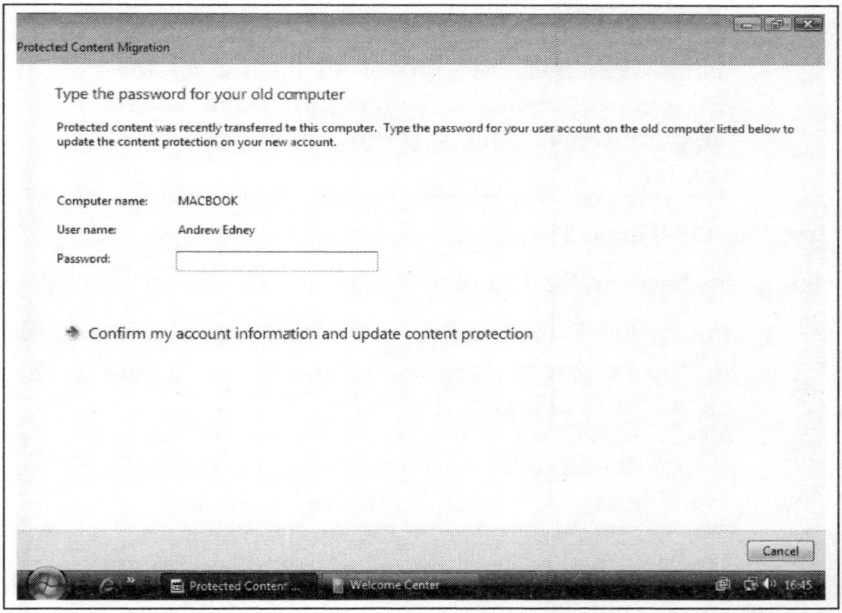

Figure 2-12 Protected Content Migration

And that is all you need to do. It is worth checking that everything is still working or in the locations that you expect your data to be stored.

Windows Vista Upgrade Advisor

If you are planning on upgrading your existing Windows operating system to Windows Vista you can run the Windows Vista Upgrade Advisor before you start the upgrade to ensure that your computer meets the minimum requirements but also that you have supported software.

> For the rest of the Upgrading section I will be using Windows XP Professional SP2 as the operating system I am upgrading from. Other supported operating systems should act in a similar way.

Installing the Windows Vista Upgrade Advisor

To do this perform the following steps:

1. Put in the Windows Vista DVD and when the Install Windows screen appears, as shown in Figure 2-13, click Check compatibility online.

> You will need to have your computer connected to the Internet in order to run this useful tool.

Figure 2-13 The Windows Vista Installation Screen

You will now be connected to the Windows Vista Upgrade Advisor website.

2. Click on the Download Windows Vista Upgrade Advisor link and then click on the Download button to start the download process. Click on Save and choose a location where you want to save the Upgrade Advisor file (such as on your desktop).

3. When the file has completed downloading, close the browser window and double-click the WindowsVistaUpgradeAdvisor.msi file and then click

on Run when you are presented with the Security Warning.

You will need to have a recent version of MSXML installed for the Upgrade Advisor to work. Don't worry if you are not sure as you will be prompted to download and install MSXML if it is not already installed. The same goes for the .Net Framework.

4. On the Welcome to the Windows Vista Upgrade Advisor Setup Wizard screen click Next.
5. Click I Agree on the License Agreement screen and click Next.
6. Choose the installation location and click Next.
7. Choose to create a desktop shortcut and click Next.

The installation will now commence.

8. Click Close to complete the installation and launch the Windows Vista Upgrade Advisor.

Running the Windows Vista Upgrade Advisor

Make sure any additional hardware you use, such as external hard drives, printers or scanners are connected before you start the scan otherwise they won't be detected!

1. After the Windows Vista Upgrade Advisor has started, click on the Start Scan button, as shown in Figure 2-14.

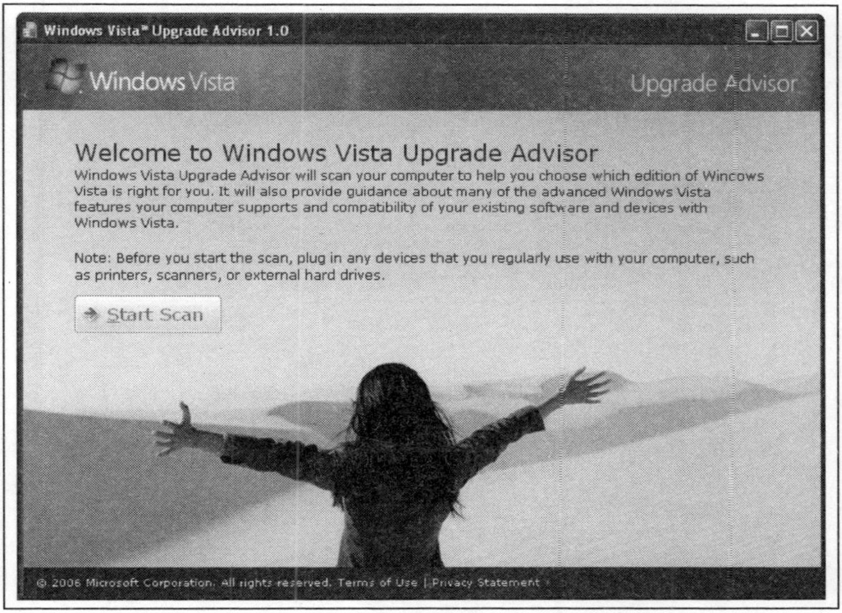

Figure 2-14 Preparing to start a scan

Whilst the scan is taking place you can click on any of the buttons on the screen to see more information about the different editions of Windows Vista, as shown in Figure 2-15.

> The system scan can take a number of minutes to complete depending on your system.

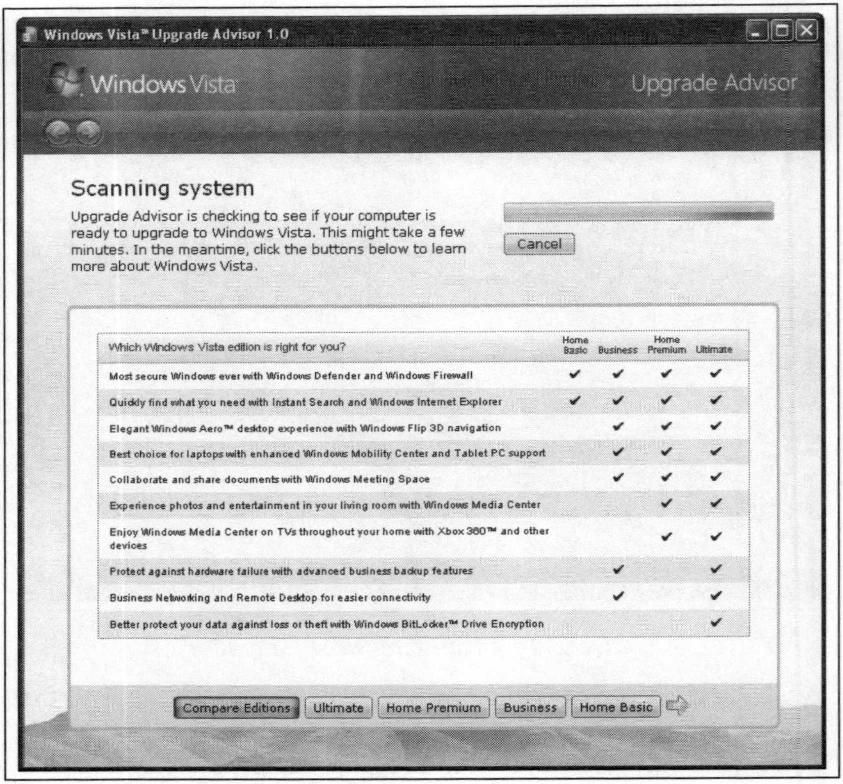

Figure 2-15 Scanning your system

2. When the system scan has completed, click on the See Details button that will appear at the top of the screen.

When the results are displayed, you will see whether or not your computer, in its current state, can run Windows Vista (as shown in Figure 2-16). You are also presented with what the advisor considers to be your best edition selection – in this case Windows Vista Business.

Figure 2-16 Windows Vista Upgrade Advisor Results

3. Read through all of the information that is presented and click on each of the See Details buttons in turn in order to review additional information that could affect the upgrade.

An example of a possible issue is shown in Figure 2-17. As you can see, the report shows that there is no compatibility data available for my Panasonic KX-P7100 printer and the advice is to visit the manufacturer's website, visit the Windows Marketplace or contact my retailer.

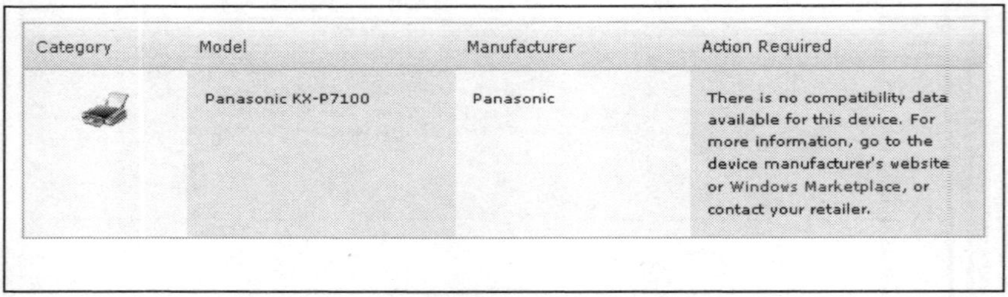

Figure 2-17 A Possible Issue for the Upgrade

Some of the issues will require you to resolve them prior to starting the upgrade process. Figure 2-18 shows an issue with the version of McAfee SecurityCenter that I have installed not being compatible with Windows Vista. The action required is to uninstall the program prior to the upgrade. But as you can see I am also told that after the upgrade has completed I won't be able to install it as it just is not compatible with Windows Vista.

You must ensure that any software you currently have that is reported as not compatible with Windows Vista is replaced with versions or other software that is. Especially in the case of AntiVirus software as you should never run a computer without adequate virus protection.

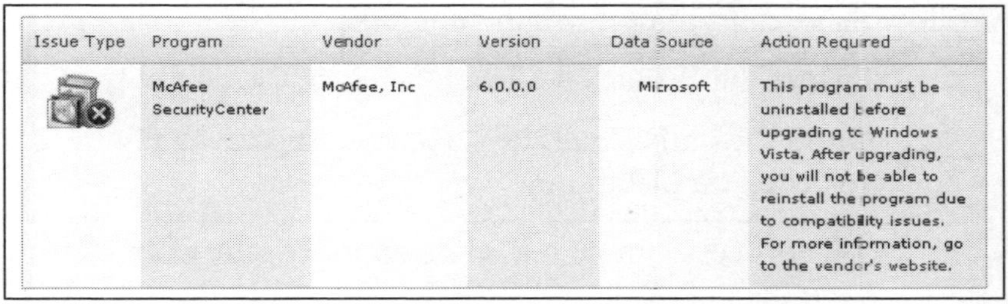

Figure 2-18 An issue that must be resolved prior to the upgrade

4. You can then print out a task list or save a report with all the actions you must perform prior to starting the installation.
5. Lastly, close down the Update Advisor and perform all the actions that are required.

Make a note of all of the software and hardware you have installed so that you can confirm everything is working correctly after the upgrade.

Performing the Upgrade

Switch off your Antivirus protection before running the upgrade as it may interfere with the process – unless of course you have already remove it as per the advice from the Upgrade Advisor.

Follow these steps to perform the upgrade:

1. Ensure the Windows Vista DVD is in the computer.
2. On the Install Windows screen (as shown in Figure 2-13) click on Install now.

   This process can take a while so make sure you have enough time put aside in order to perform the upgrade.

3. On the Get important updates for installation screen, as shown in Figure 2-19, double-click Go online to get the latest updates for installation. This should make the installation process smoother.

   The computer will need to remain connected to the Internet for the duration of the upgrade.

4. Enter your Product Key for the edition of Windows Vista you have purchased. By default, Windows will automatically be activated when you are online. If for whatever reason you don't want this to happen, just untick the box. Click next to continue.

5. Read the licence terms and tick the I accept the licence terms box, followed by clicking Next.

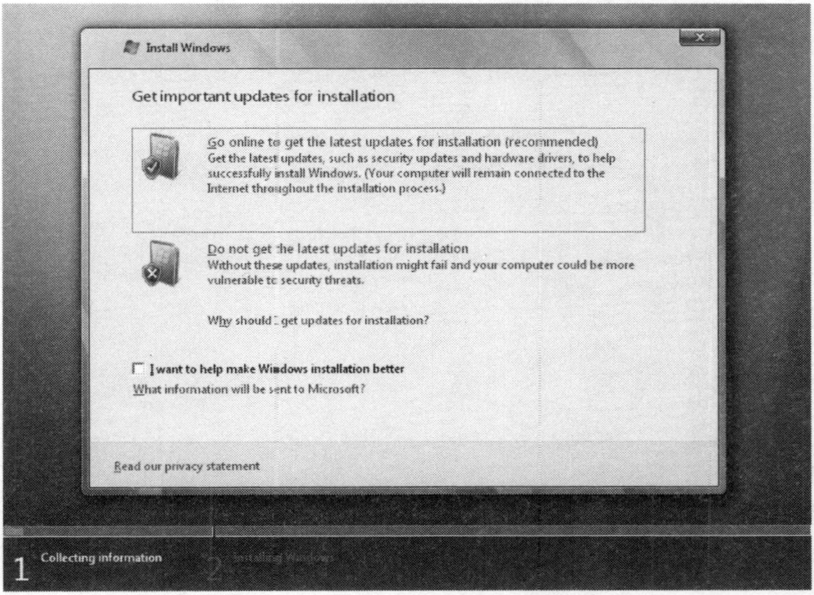

Figure 2-19 Getting important updates for installation

6. The next screen asks which type of installation you want to perform, as shown in Figure 2-20. Click Upgrade to keep your files, settings and programs. If you would prefer to install a clean copy of Windows Vista at this point click Custom instead.

7. You may see a Compatibility Report at this stage. As long as the issues do not prevent the upgrade you can just click on Next to continue.

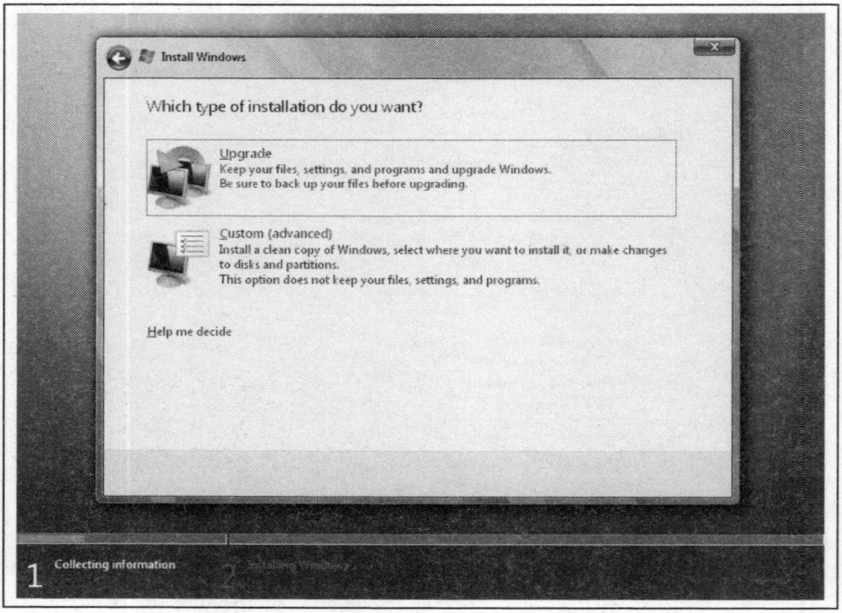

Figure 2-20 Choosing which type of installation to perform

The upgrade will now commence, as shown in Figure 2-21. At this point all you can do is wait while the upgrade takes place, remembering that it could take several hours to complete depending on your system.

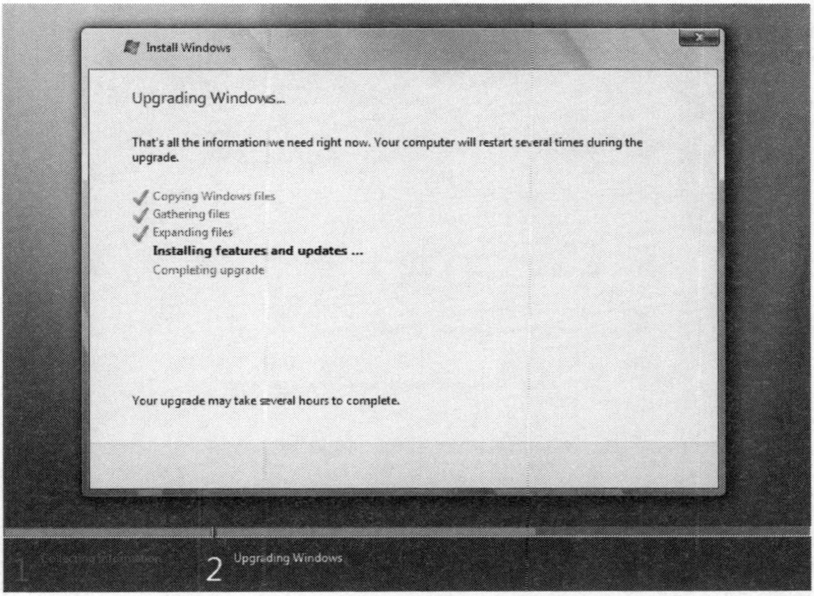

Figure 2-21 Upgrading Windows

8. You will then be asked to choose how you want to protect Windows automatically, as shown in Figure 2-22. The options are:

    - Use recommended settings (which will install all important and recommended updates, help make Internet browsing safer, and check online for solutions to problems)

    - Install important updates only (which only installs security updates and other important Windows updates)

- Ask me later (which does nothing for now)

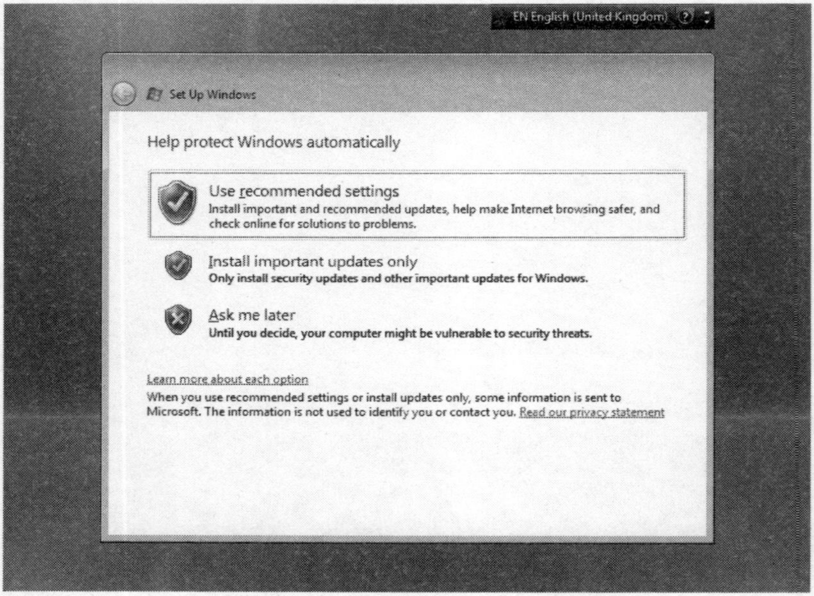

Figure 2-22 Deciding how to protect Windows

It is certainly advisable to select the Use recommended settings option to ensure you are always up to date in order to reduce any security or application problems.

9. Review your time and date settings and click Next.
10. You must then select your computer's current location, as shown in Figure 2-23. This is so that Windows can

automatically apply the correct network settings for the location you are in.

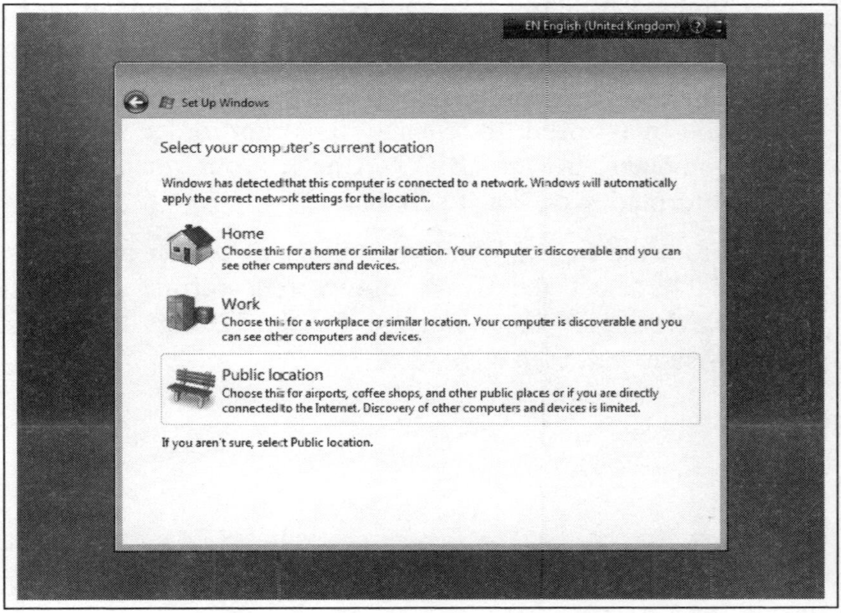

Figure 2-23 Selecting your computer's current location

11. And that's it. All that is left to do now is click the Start button and Windows Vista awaits.

Windows Vista will now check your computer's performance. This may take a few minutes, so be patient, not long now.

A Clean Install

1. Put the Windows Vista DVD in the computer and switch the computer on.
2. The computer should boot from the DVD – if it doesn't you may need to change the boot order of your computer in the BIOS. Check your manual for information on how to do this.
3. From the Install Windows screen, as shown in Figure 2-24, select the Time and current format and the Keyboard or input method for the settings that you wish to use, then click next.

Figure 2-24 Selecting the Language, Time and Keyboard settings

4. Click on the Install now button, as shown in Figure 2-25.

Figure 2-25 Starting the installation

5. Enter your Product Key for the edition of Windows Vista you have purchased, as shown in Figure 2-26. By default, Windows will automatically be activated when you are online. If for whatever reason you don't want this to happen, just un-tick the box. Click next to continue.

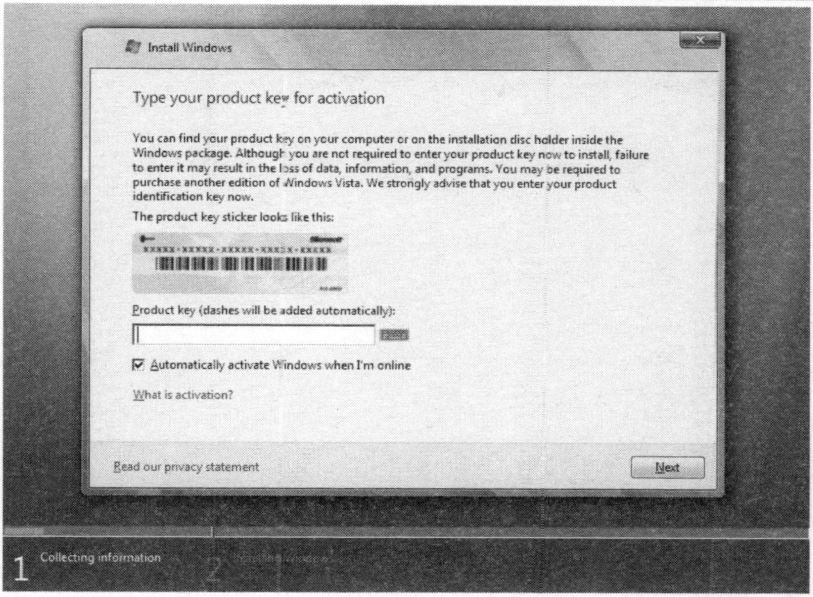

Figure 2-26 Entering your Product Key

6. Read the licence terms and tick the I accept the licence terms box, followed by clicking Next.

7. You will then see the installation selection screen, as shown in Figure 2-27. You will notice that the Upgrade option has been disabled because this a completely clean installation on a formatted hard drive. Click on Custom (advanced).

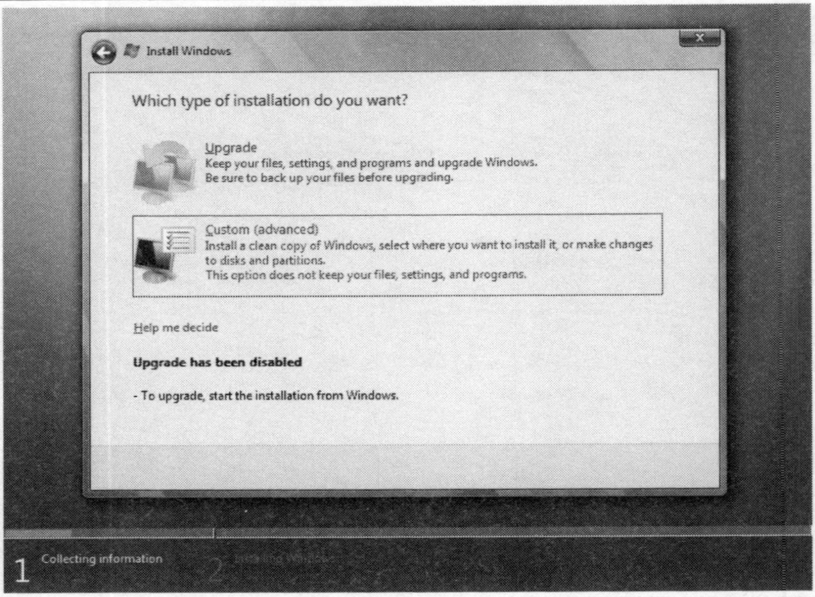

Figure 2-27 Installation Selection

8. You can now select where you want to install Windows Vista, as shown in Figure 2-28. Click on Drive Options and select New to create a new partition.
9. Select the size of the partition you want to use then click Apply.

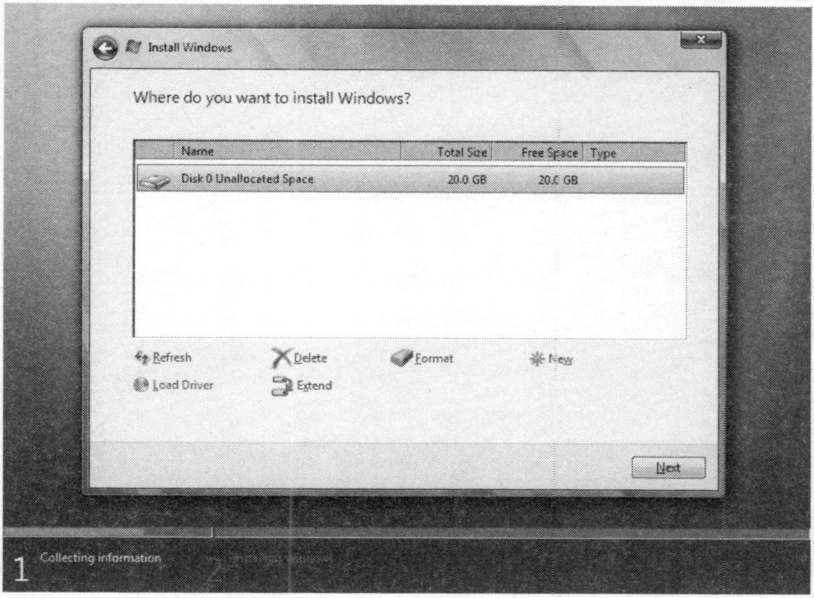

Figure 2-28 Creating drive partitions

10. Click Next to begin installing Windows Vista, as shown in Figure 2-29.

The installation process can take some time to complete – be patient.

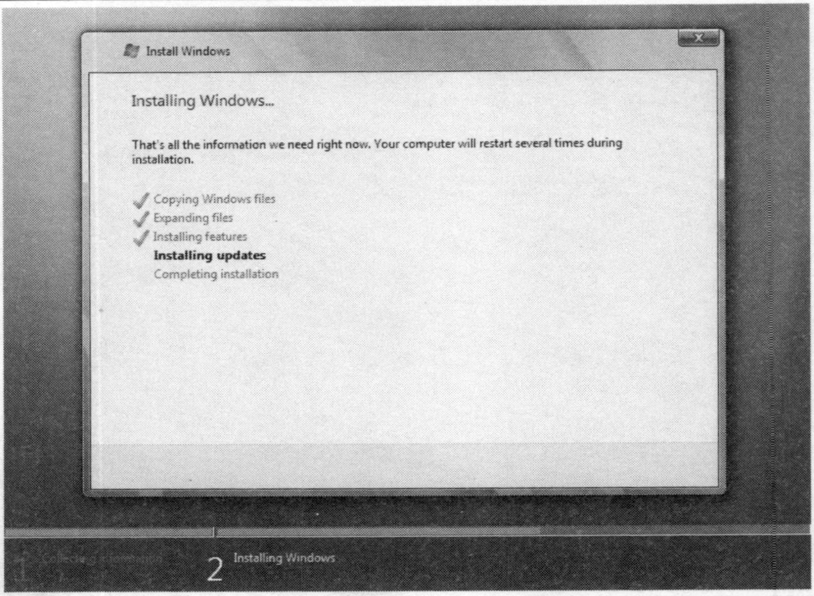

Figure 2-29 Installing Windows Vista

11. After Windows Vista has installed, you will be prompted to choose a username and enter a password, as shown in Figure 2-30. Entering a password is optional but I highly recommend you enter one. You can also enter a password hint for those times that you forget what your password is. Also you can select a picture for your user account from one of the many pictures available. Click Next when you are done.

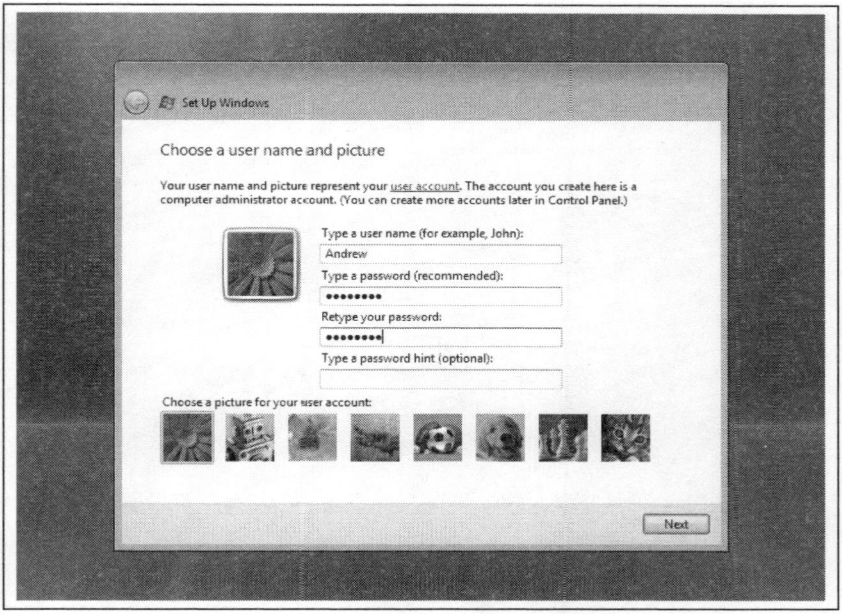

Figure 2-30 Entering a username and password and selecting a picture

12. The next step is to enter a name for the computer and to select a suitable background, as shown in Figure 2-31. You can enter anything you like for the ccmputer name.

Try to name your computer with something meaningful – especially if you have multiple computers.

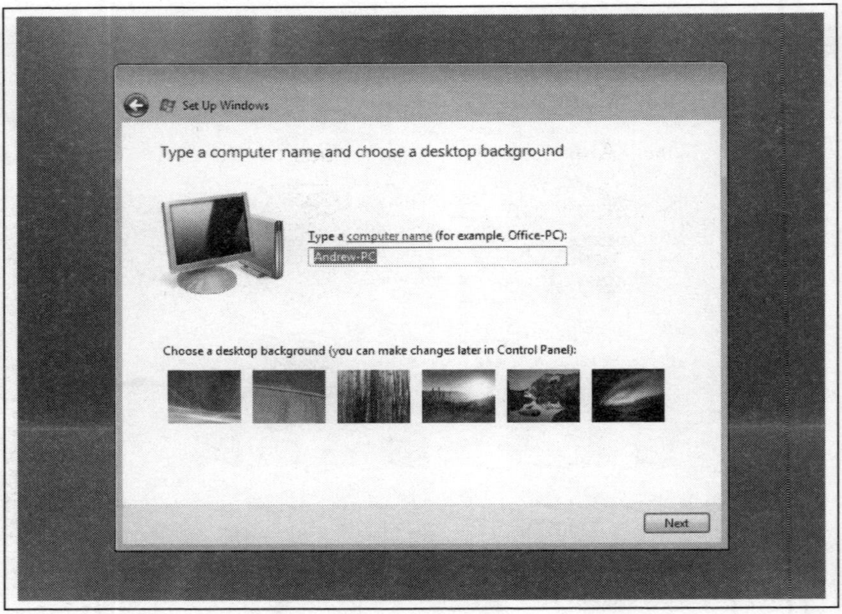

Figure 2-31 Entering a computer name and choosing a background

13. You will then be asked to choose how you want to protect Windows automatically, as shown in Figure 2-32. The options are:

    - Use recommended settings (which will install all important and recommended updates, help make Internet browsing safer, and check online for solutions to problems)

- Install important updates only (which only installs security updates and other important Windows updates)
- Ask me later (which does nothing for now)

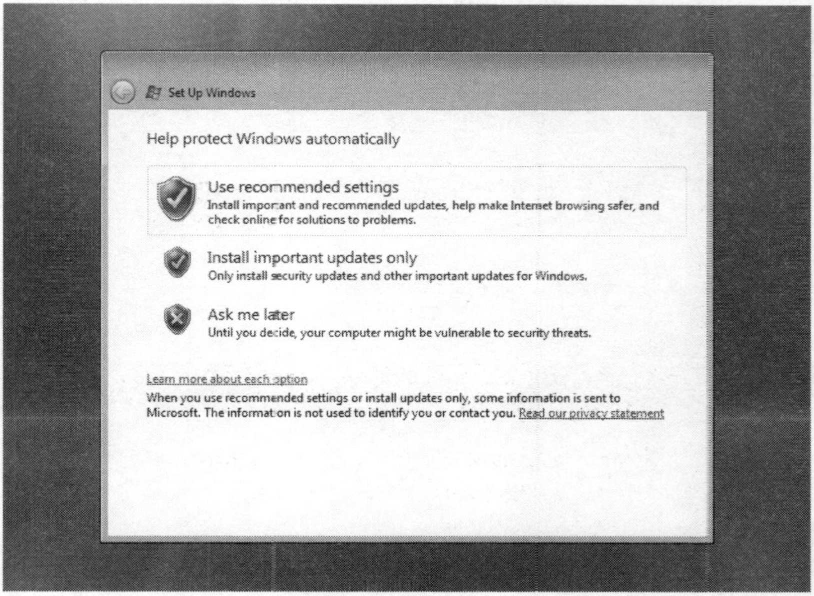

Figure 2-32 Deciding how to protect Windows

It is certainly advisable to select the Use recommended settings option to ensure you are always up to date in order to reduce any security or application problems.

14. You must then select which time zone you are in and also set the date and the time, as shown in Figure 2-33. Click Next to continue.

If the date and time are set correctly in the BIOS of your computer this should be reflected here.

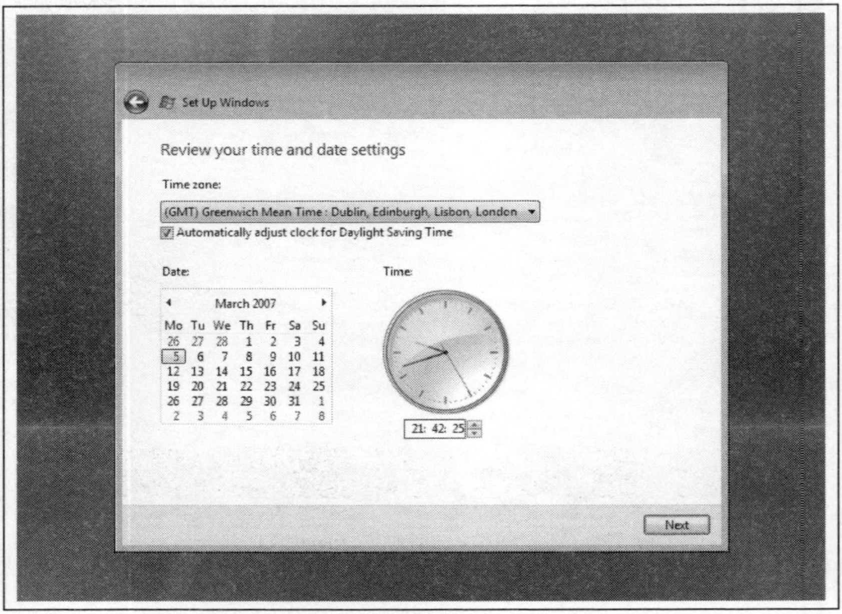

Figure 2-33 Setting the date and time

The following step may not appear if your network card requires additional drivers to work with Windows Vista.

---

15. You must then select your computer's current location, as shown in Figure 2-34. This is so that Windows can automatically apply the correct network settings for the location you are in.

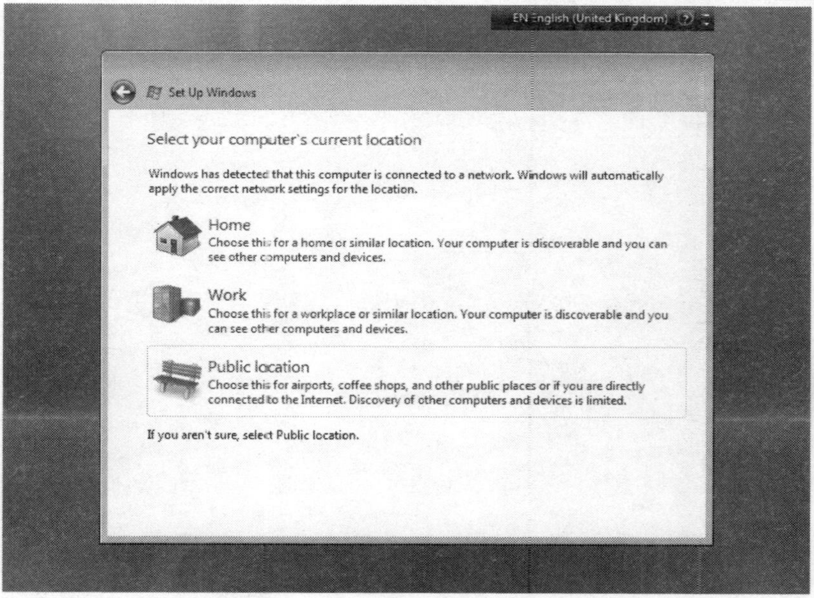

Figure 2-34 Selecting your computer's current location

16. And that's it. All that is left to do now is click the Start button and Windows Vista awaits.

Windows Vista will now check your computer's performance. This may take a few minutes, so be patient, not long now.

Post Installation Tasks

Now that the installation has completed, you will need to sign into your user account, as shown in Figure 2-35.

Figure 2-35 Signing into your user account

You won't have to do this if you decided you didn't want to use a password.

You should now check that all of your hardware is functioning correctly. To do this you can look at the Device Manager, as shown in Figure 2-36. As you can see I need to install an updated driver for my Multimedia Audio Controller.

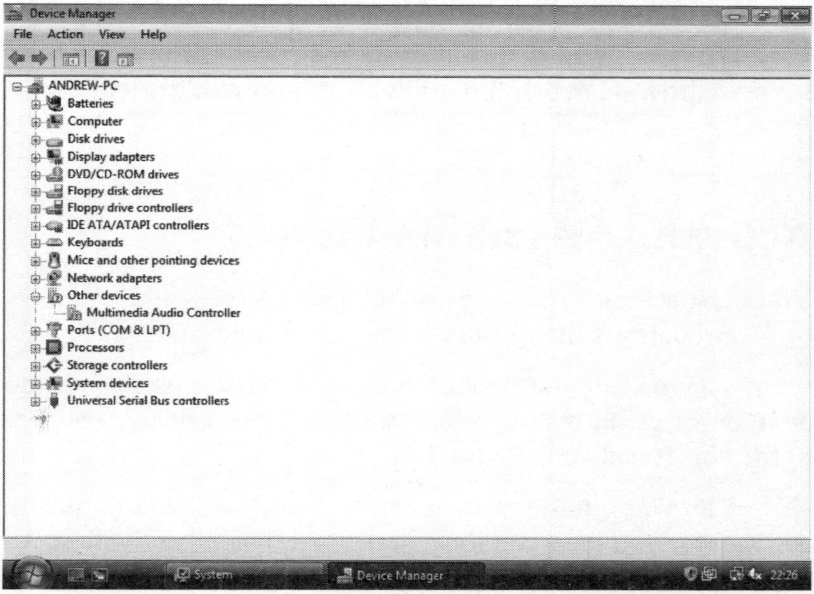

Figure 2-36 Checking hardware in Device Manager

1. Click on View Computer Details from the Welcome Center.
2. Click Show more details.
3. Click on Device Manager from the Tasks list on the left-hand part of the window.
4. Check that all the devices are listed without warnings or errors and install any updates or additional drivers wherever necessary.

Remember what the Upgrade Advisor told you about supported hardware – some of your hardware may not work with Windows Vista.

Activating Windows Vista

You must activate your copy of Windows Vista within 30 days or functionality will stop and Vista will be unusable.

If you left the default activation setting on during the upgrade or clean install, Windows will automatically connect to Microsoft and activate for you.

If you chose not to have Windows automatically activate for you then you must perform a manual activation.

To do this, perform the following steps:

You must be connected to the Internet for activation to be successful, so ensure you have your network card functioning or you are connected to your Wireless network before proceeding.

1. Click on View Computer Details from the Welcome Center.
2. Click Show more details.

3. Check at the bottom of the screen within the Windows activation area to see if your copy of Windows Vista has been activated, as shown in Figure 2-37.

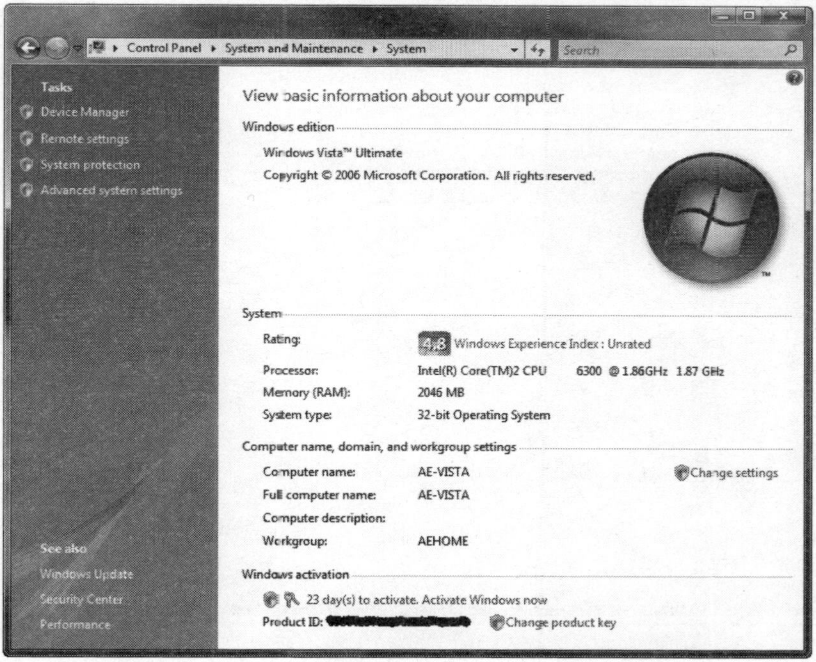

Figure 2-37 Checking on activation

As you can see from Figure 2-37 my copy of Windows needs to be activated within 23 days.

4. Click on Activate Windows now to begin the activation process.

5. Click on Activate Windows online now.

6. Assuming activation was successful, you should see the screen shown in Figure 2-38.

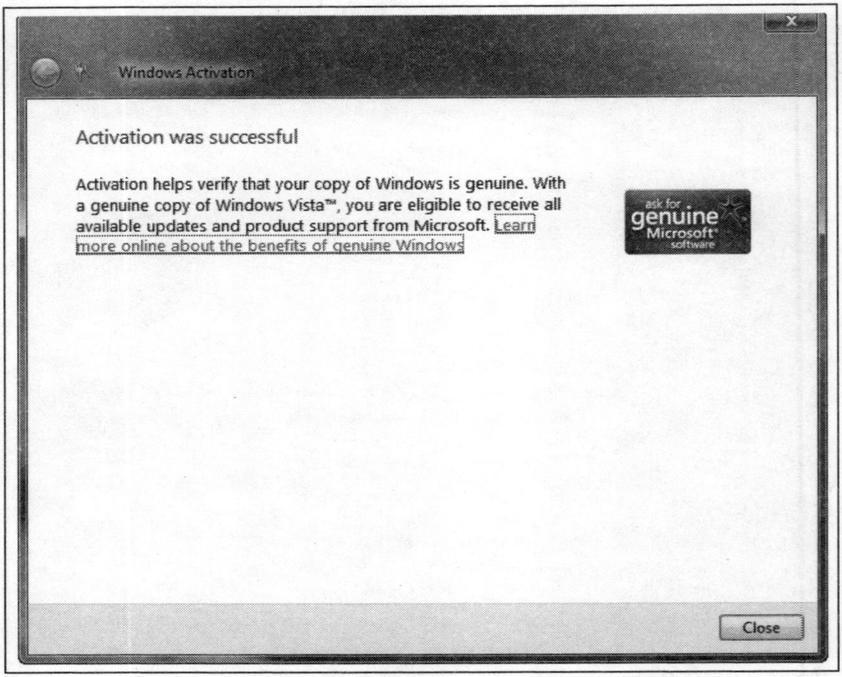

Figure 2-38 Activation successfully completed

Activation failures could be as a result of network problems or even trying to activate an illegal copy of Windows Vista.

7. Click Close to finish.

You should now see that Windows is activated.

Windows Anytime Upgrade

Depending on the edition of Windows Vista you have installed, you may have the opportunity to upgrade it to a different edition from within the operating system itself.

You can upgrade the following:

- Home Basic to Home Premium
- Home Basic to Ultimate
- Home Premium to Ultimate
- Business to Ultimate

This is called the Windows Anytime Upgrade. You can see if you have this opportunity by doing the following:

1. Click on View Computer Details from the Welcome Center.
2. Click Show more details.
3. If you can upgrade, it should be visible under Windows edition, as shown in Figure 2-39.

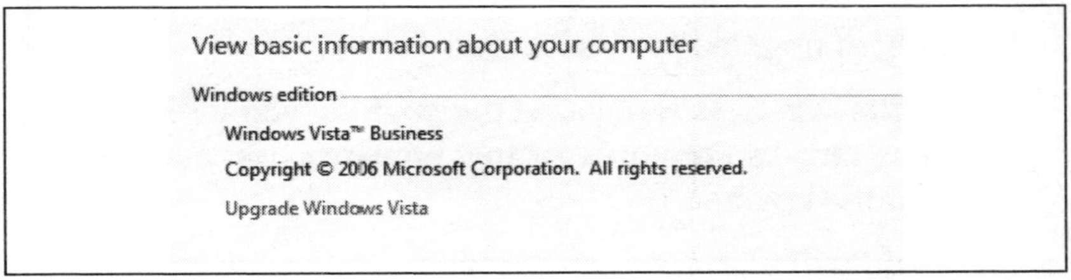

Figure 2-39 Checking if you can upgrade Vista editions

4. Click on Upgrade Windows Vista to launch the Windows Anytime Upgrade screen, as shown in Figure 2-40.
5. Click on Upgrade to Windows Vista Ultimate (or whichever edition you want to upgrade to).

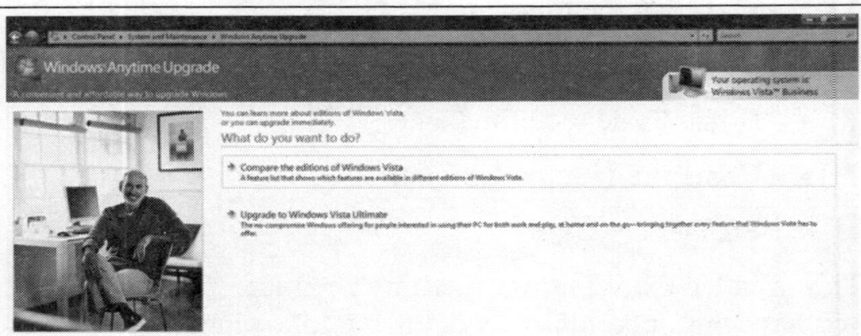

Figure 2-40 Windows Anytime Upgrade

Before you can continue this process, your copy of Windows Vista needs to have been activated.

---

6. You need to purchase the Windows Vista Upgrade Online as shown in Figure 2-41. To do this click on the Begin upgrade process button.
7. After you have purchased the upgrade you will need to download some software that prepares your computer for the upgrade.
8. You will then need your Windows Anytime Upgrade disc. Don't worry if you don't have one, you can easily order one from the Microsoft website

https://emea.windowsanytimeupgradestore.com/WAU_DIRECT/Purchase.aspx.

9. Follow the onscreen instructions to perform the upgrade.

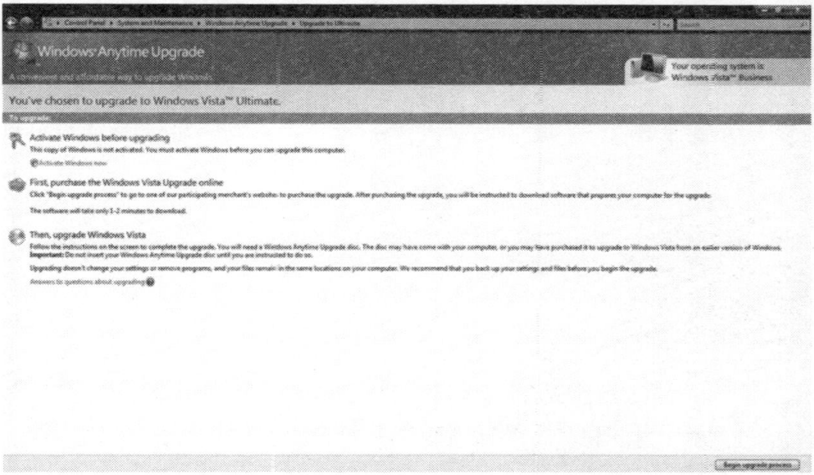

Figure 2-41 Purchasing the Windows Vista Upgrade Online

Don't forget that your computer must be capable of running the newly chosen edition of Windows Vista so make sure you have checked this prior to buying the upgrade, just in case.

PART 3
Getting the Most From Windows Vista

3

The New Desktop

Obviously the first thing you will notice about Windows Vista is that the desktop is new, and while it looks similar to Windows XP, it clearly isn't!

This chapter will take a very brief look at the new desktop, including the updated Start Menu, Windows Explorer and the new Aero system.

The Start Menu

If you have used any previous version of Windows then you will be familiar with the Start Menu. This is the place you go to in order to start applications or tasks, shut down the computer, and so on. Unlike previous versions, as you work your way through the items on the menu, all the results are displayed within the menu itself rather than opening additional windows.

One major advantage over previous versions of the Start Menu is the ability to search for a specific application or file without the need to work your way through the menu system. There is a box labeled Start Search, as shown in Figure 3-1, and you just have to enter something there and any results will be displayed for you.

Figure 3-1 The Start Menu

As you type the text into the box, Windows Vista will check filenames, metadata and the full text in files for you so that nothing should get missed. You just then select the file or application and it's as simple as that.

> You can add applications or shortcuts to the Start Menu and customise it however you wish.

Explorer

This is not to be confused with Internet Explorer. Vista Explorer is a tool for searching or, viewing and managing all sorts of information, pictures, applications and more. Again, it's the bigger and better version of the previous Windows Explorer.

The Explorer window, as shown in Figure 3-2, is broken up into a number of different sections, including:

- Instant Search – enabling you to just enter some text and see the results.
- Navigation pane – enabling you to just click on a link or item in a folder.
- Command bar – a single place for all useful commands, such as changing views, running slide shows, opening documents, and so on.
- Live icons – these are very useful for applications that support this feature. What this does is provide a thumbnail preview of the contents of the file, rather than just a thumbnail icon.

- Details pane – provides information on the file, such as size, date, etc.
- Preview pane – provides the ability to preview the content of a file, without actually having to open it.

Figure 3-2 A view of a folder in Explorer

Aero

Windows Aero is described as the premium visual experience of Windows Vista. It also features something referred to as Aero Glass which is a transparent glass effect on the borders of windows and also includes new subtle animations and colours.

> Aero is included with the following Windows Vista editions: Business, Enterprise, Home Premium and Ultimate.

As well as running one of the versions of Windows Vista that supports Aero, you must have a graphics card that supports the Windows Display Driver Model (WDDM).

> Check that your graphics card meets all the requirements for both Windows Vista and Aero.

You can easily change the colours by going to the Control Panel and selecting Customise Colours, as shown in Figure 3-3.

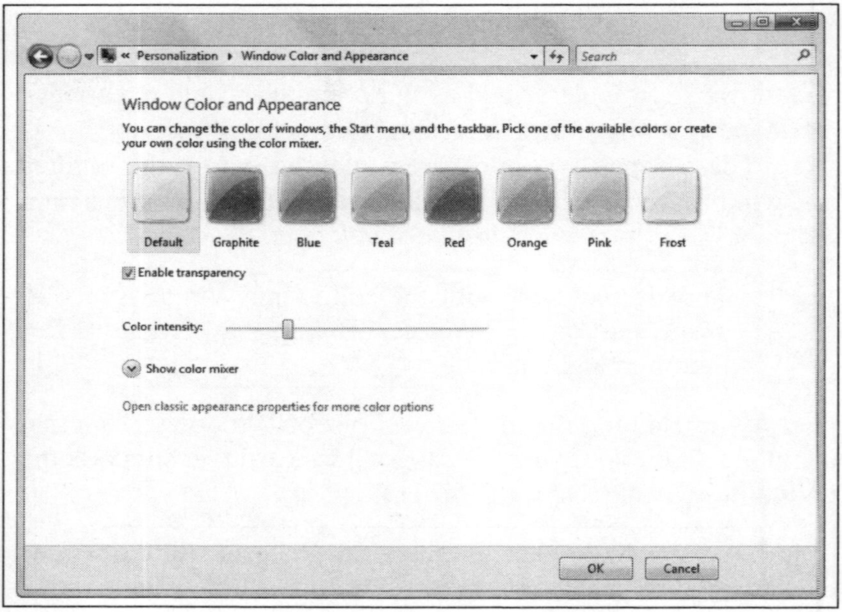

Figure 3-3 Customising the colours

Flip

Flip is the new enhanced way of swapping between open windows. Instead of the way it was done in the old days where you could only see an icon for the application you had open, you now see thumbnails of your open windows in a single location, as shown in Figure 3-4.

Figure 3-4 Flipping through open windows

You can flip through the open windows by using the ALT and TAB keys. When you release the keys on a highlighted window, that window will open up.

Flip 3D

Flip 3D is a cool new feature with Windows Aero that enables you to quickly preview all of your open Windows in a 3D way without the need to switch to each Window, as shown in Figure 3-5.

You can start the Flip 3D process at any time by clicking on the Switch between windows icon in the taskbar. You can then use the wheel on your mouse (if you have one) to scroll between the windows and make a selection. You can also use the arrows on your keyboard to do the same thing.

> You can also start the Flip 3D process by pressing the Windows key on the keyboard followed by the TAB key.

Figure 3-5 Using Flip 3D to view open windows

Other Improvements

There are also a vast number of other improvements over previous versions of Windows, and even though they may not have the same impact as something like Aero, they are still useful.

ClearType

ClearType was introduced with Windows XP and was designed to provide a clearer text image on your monitor in order to make it easier to read. In Windows XP ClearType was not switched on by default and so users had to specifically switch it on – and a lot of users didn't even know it was there.

With Windows Vista, ClearType is switched on by default so users are automatically gaining the benefits of it!

Dialog Boxes

Well we are all used to seeing dialog boxes appear, and in Windows Vista they are still there. However, the dialog boxes have been redesigned to be larger, more informative and easier to read and understand. You should be able to determine exactly what is needed to be done or what a dialog box actually means, more so than with previous versions.

Wizards

Wizards are great for helping you to perform certain tasks and guiding you through procedures such as connecting to the Internet. Similar to dialog boxes, there are more wizards to help you and the wizards themselves are clearer, contain more graphics and explanations and so on the whole are much easier to understand and use.

Summary

Even though this chapter is quite short, you should have now seen that there are lots of improvements to the desktop with Windows Vista. Windows Aero is by far the best improvement, but you must have both a supported version of Windows Vista and a supported graphics card.

4

Personalisation

Windows Vista provides a unique experience for different users and for different computers. Most of this experience is configurable, although some isn't, and that is usually down to both the version of Windows Vista being used and also the available hardware in the computer that is being used.

This chapter will take a look at some of the applications and components that can be used to create a personalised experience, the Windows Sidebar and Gadgets and the Windows Experience Index.

Windows Experience Index

Whilst not specifically used to personalise your Windows Vista experience, using the Windows Experience Index can help you to understand your computer's capabilities and limitations.

The Windows Experience Index is used to measure the capability of the computer you are using, including both the hardware and the software. The measurement is then presented as a number, known as the Base Score. The base score is actually the lowest score of all the components tested. So effectively your base score could be very low because of low memory and it could easily be raised by adding more memory.

Each of the results can score between 1 and 5.9.

Table 4-1 shows the components that are tested and what is actually rated.

Component	**What Is Rated**
Processor	Calculations per second
Memory (RAM)	Memory operations per second
Graphics	Desktop performance for Windows Aero
Gaming Graphics	3D business and gaming graphics performance
Primary hard disk	Disk data transfer rate

Table 4-1 Tested components

You can run the tests again to update your score at any time. You should do this as a matter of course if you change a component in your computer system.

To run the tests, go to the Performance Information and Tools screen, which can be accessed by selecting Windows Experience Index from the System screen.

You can view your current rating from here, as shown in Figure 4-1.

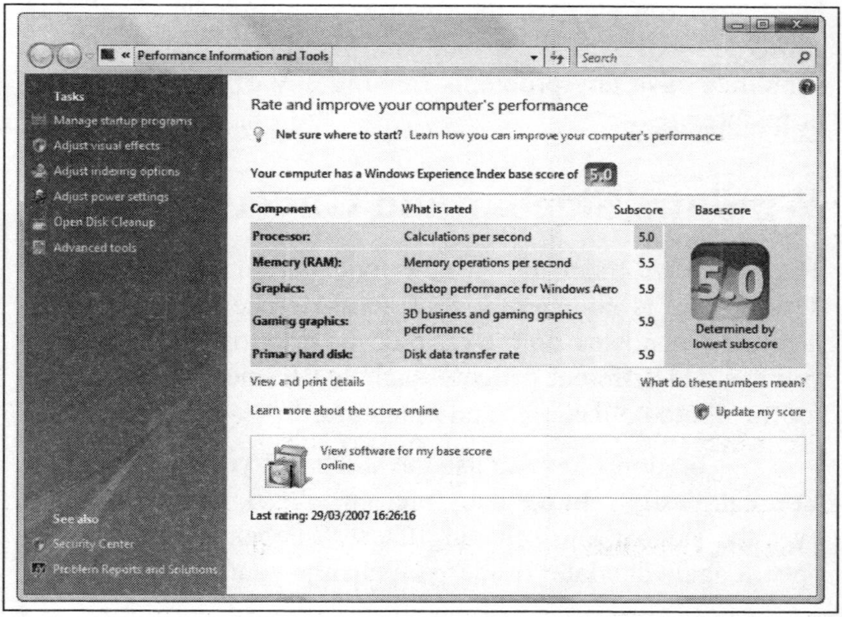

Figure 4-1 Windows Experience Index

You can see from the example in Figure 4-1, my base score is 5.0 because of my processor.

To update the score, just click on the Update my score link.

The tests can take a few minutes so be patient.

If any of the subscores are less than 2 then you really do need to think about replacing that component.

If you have a subscore of 3 or above then you should be able to run most of the features of Windows Vista. Any subscore above 5 is perfect for Windows Vista and you shouldn't have any problems running any of the applications or features.

Windows Sidebar and Gadgets

The Windows Sidebar is a new tool that sits nicely on your desktop and is completely configurable. The sidebar itself is just that – a sidebar on the edge of the desktop. In this sidebar you can add different gadgets, such as RSS newsfeeds, clocks, rolling photo collections, and much more.

You don't have to use the sidebar if you don't want to. You can easily remove it by pressing the right mouse button over the sidebar and selecting Close Sidebar. You can easily open it again at a later time if you change your mind.

As mentioned earlier, gadgets are applications that you can have running on the sidebar. Windows Vista ships with a number of gadgets to choose from, and you can also download new ones.

Figure 4-2 shows the Windows Sidebar with a number of gadgets running, including a clock and the RSS newsfeeds.

Figure 4-2 The Windows Sidebar and Gadgets

You can easily add gadgets to the sidebar by right-clicking on the sidebar and choosing Add Gadgets from the menu.

You will then see the Gadget Gallery, as shown in Figure 4-3. You can then choose one of the gadgets to add to the sidebar by double-clicking it. You can then move it to a position on the sidebar that you are happy with.

You can also search for gadgets or even click on the Get more gadgets online link to see hundreds more gadgets you can choose from, such as the clock I have on my screen in the style of the popular TV show 24.

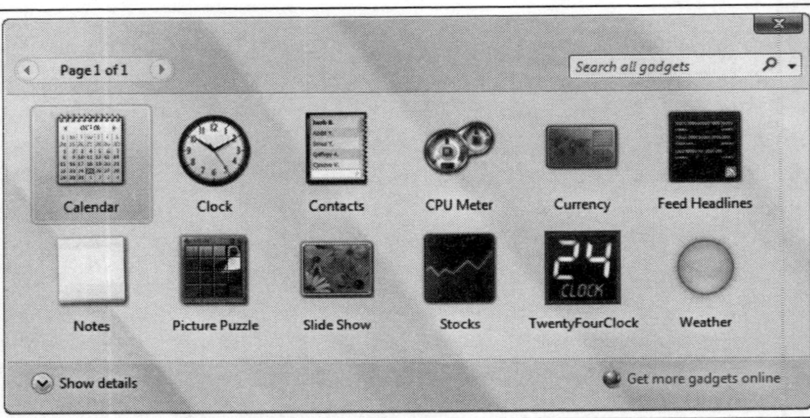

Figure 4-3 The Gadget Gallery

If you want to remove a gadget from the sidebar, just hover over it and click the X. You will then be asked to confirm you want to close it, as shown in Figure 4-4, just click on Close Gadget.

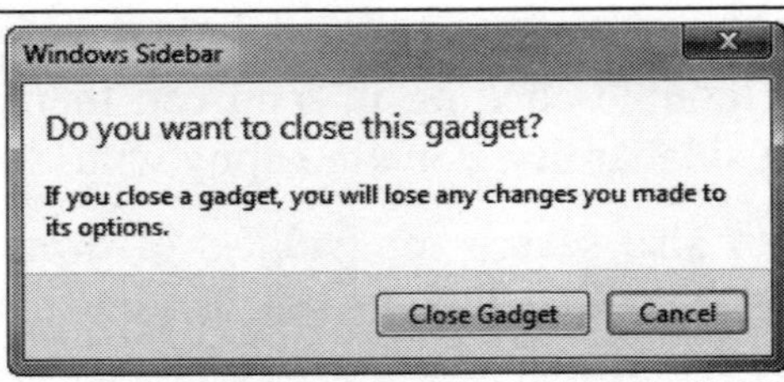

Figure 4-4 Confirming closing a gadget

Summary

Obviously one of the great things about Windows has always been that you can configure and personalise Windows to pretty much however you want it. This chapter has only provided you with a brief look at some of the new ways to personalise your experience – believe me, there are plenty more available, you just need to go and play around in Windows and make it your own.

5

Useful Tools and Applications

There are a number of very useful tools and applications provided straight out of the box with Windows Vista. This chapter will describe some of the more useful ones, including the Welcome Center, Windows Backup and Restore and Control Panel. Some of the tools and applications you may use more than others, and some you may decide never to use – the choice is yours. If you find a tool or application useful then use it, if not there are probably plenty of other ways to do what you need. That's one of the great things about Windows Vista, there are usually a number of different tools that do similar things depending on how you like to operate.

Welcome Center

The Welcome Center is the first thing that any user will see when they log into Windows Vista. The Welcome Center was designed so that users would have a single place to go in order to complete a number of tasks that are typically required the first time you use Windows. These tasks include connecting to the Internet, adding new users, transferring files and settings (as you recall from Chapter 2), and more. Figure 5-1 shows the Welcome Center screen that will be displayed.

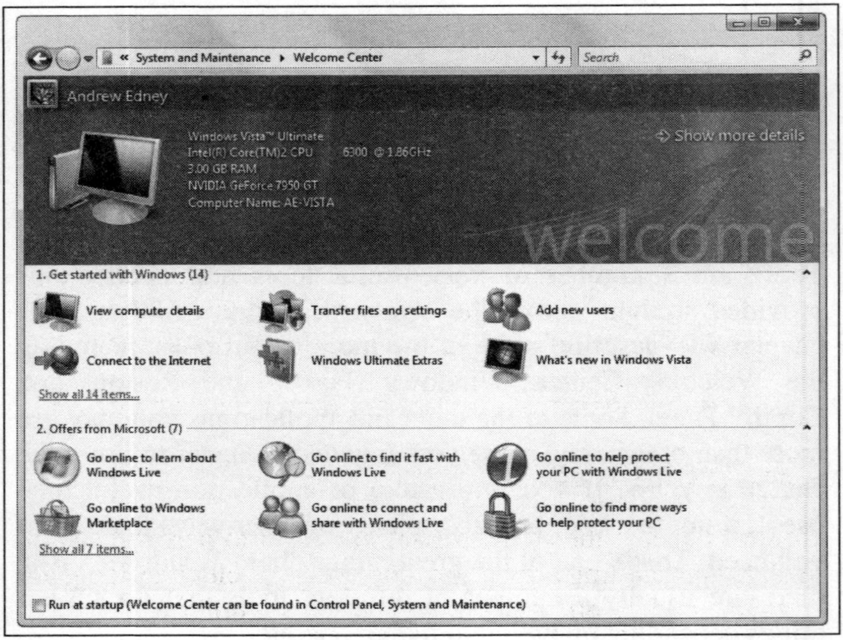

Figure 5-1 The Welcome Center

Other information that is visible includes the name of the account you are logged in as, the version of Vista you are using (in this case, Ultimate), various details on the specification of the computer and the computer name. There are also a number of offers from Microsoft included if you want to take any of them, including various Windows Live offers.

Depending on the size of your screen, you may not be able to see all of the items, in which case you will see a link that says something similar to "show all 14 items". If you click the link the additional items will be displayed.

To perform any of the tasks, just click on them and follow the on-screen instructions. When you have completed all the tasks you want, and that may take several days or weeks (as some of the tasks you may be in no rush to complete) you can choose not to have the Welcome Screen displayed again. To do this, just remove the tick from the Run at Startup box.

> You can launch the Welcome Center at any time, even if you have chosen not to run at startup.

Control Panel

Control Panel is the place to go if you want to perform actions such as uninstalling a program, changing the clock or language settings or many other tasks, as shown in Figure 5-2.

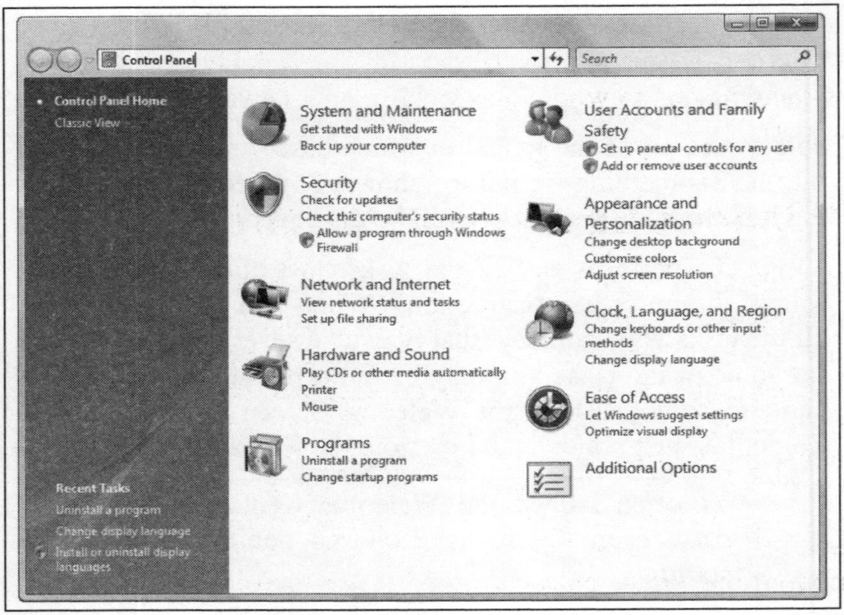

Figure 5-2 Windows Vista Control Panel

The Control Panel has be redesigned to give it a consistent look with the rest of Windows Vista and as such is very intuitive and easy to use.

If you prefer to use the old style for Control Panel, click on the Classic View link.

You can either click on the main headings to open up each of them and then make your selection, or you can click on one of the tasks under each heading if what you want to do is listed.

You will also see a list of Recent Tasks shown in the bottom left corner of the screen so that you can quickly repeat tasks without having to work your way through the various available options.

Windows Backup and Restore

We all know how important it is to make backups of our important files just in case something happens and we need to restore them. And we all know that feeling when we haven't backed them up and something does happen. Well the excuse of it being too difficult, or not having the correct software is now a thing of the past with Windows Backup and Restore.

You can easily choose which files you want to backup and restore and you can choose where you want to back them up to, for example onto DVD or CD, an external hard drive or even to another computer on your network. All this takes place from the Windows Backup and Restore Center.

> Programs and system files are not included in the backup and so if you want to backup those you should look to use something else unless you are using Vista Business, Enterprise or Ultimate which includes the ability to perform a full backup and restore.

To launch the Windows Backup and Restore Center, as shown in Figure 5-3, go to Control Panel and select the Backup your computer link from the System and Maintenance area.

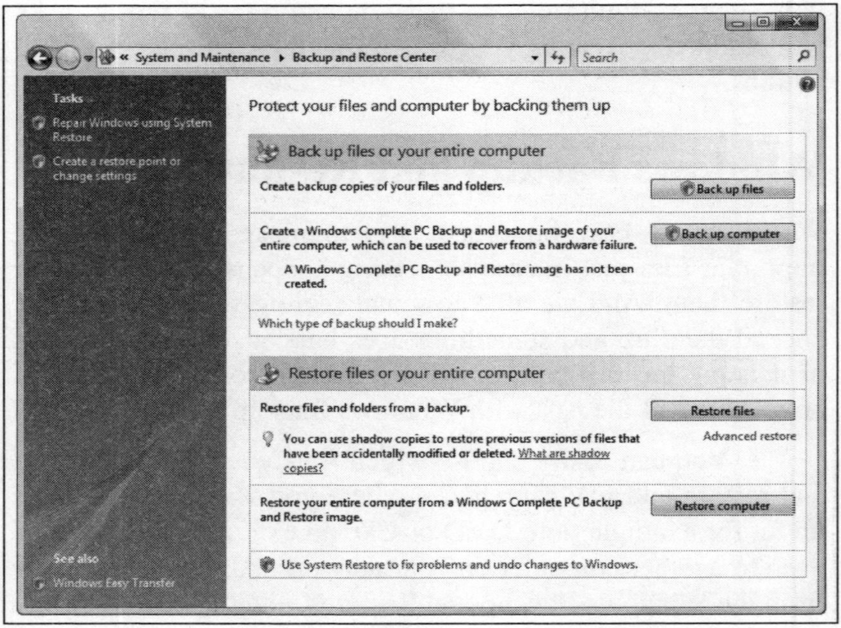

Figure 5-3 The Backup and Restore Center

As you can see, the Backup and Restore Center is split into two main areas – Backup and Restore, making it very simple to use.

Performing a Backup

Performing a backup is simple, and all you need to do is follow these few steps:

1. From the Backup and Restore Center, click the Back up files button.

   If you have User Access Control enabled on your computer you will need to give your permission to continue.

2. You will then need to select where you want to save your backup, as shown in Figure 5-4, then click Next.

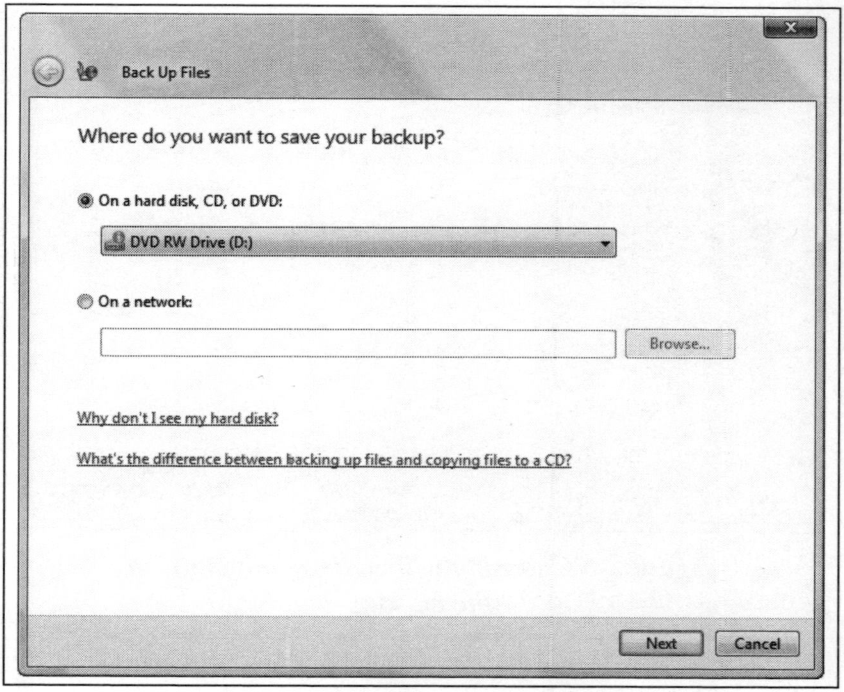

Figure 5-4 Choosing a backup location

3. If you have more than one hard disc in your computer you will be asked which discs you want to include in the backup, as shown in Figure 5-5. Choose the discs and then click Next to continue.

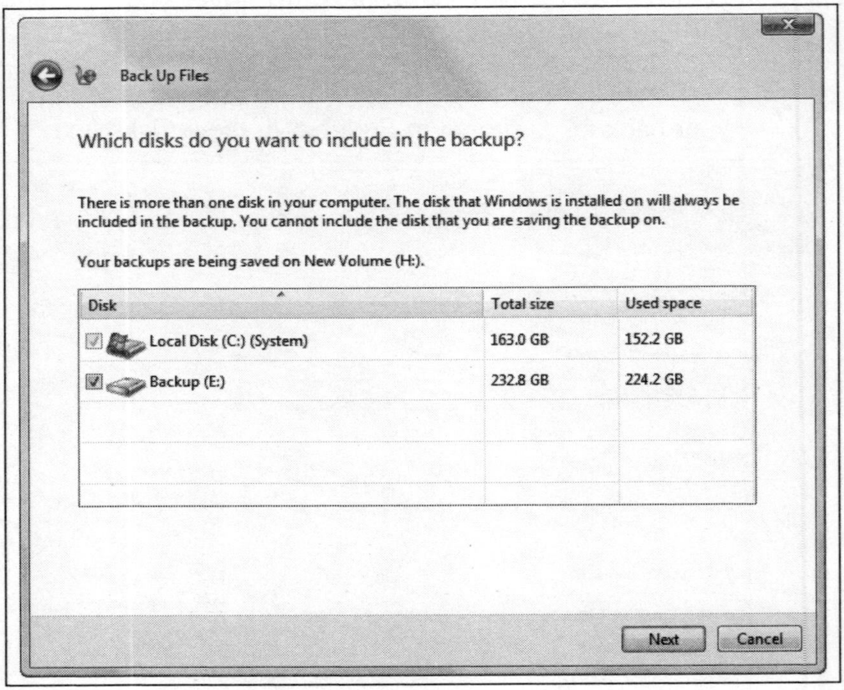

Figure 5-5 Choosing which discs to include in the backup

If you selected to save your backups to a hard drive, you will not be able to include that drive in the actual backup process.

4. You will then be asked to confirm which file types you want to back up from a list, as shown in Figure 5-6.

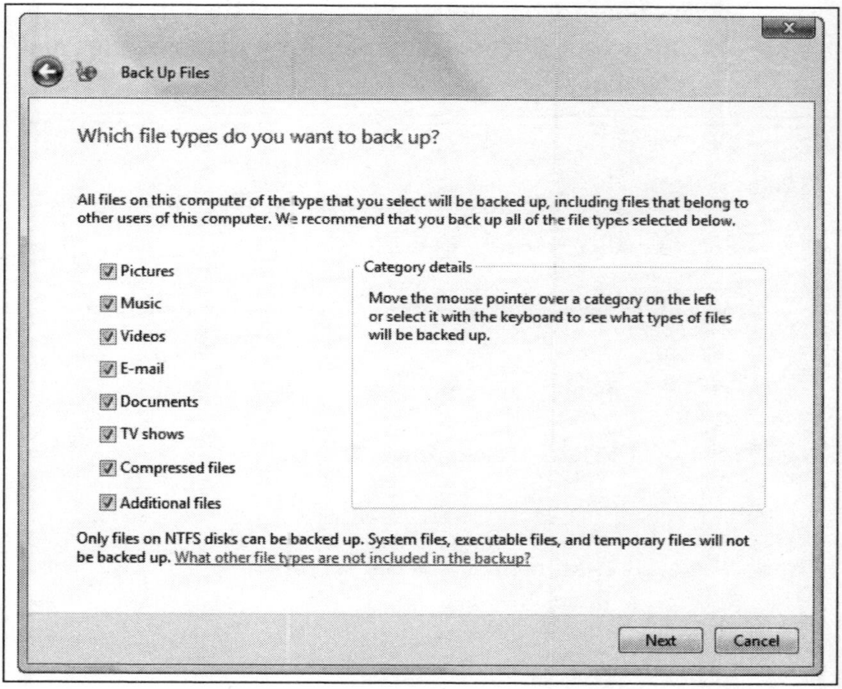

Figure 5-6 Choosing the types of files to backup

Don't forget the more you choose, the bigger the backup will be and so the longer it will take to perform, not to mention the more backup media that will be required (unless you are backing up to another computer or hard drive).

5. So that you never forget to do another backup, you can set how often you want the backup performed, and even choose what day and time, as shown in Figure 5-7. Make your selections and click on Save settings and start backup.

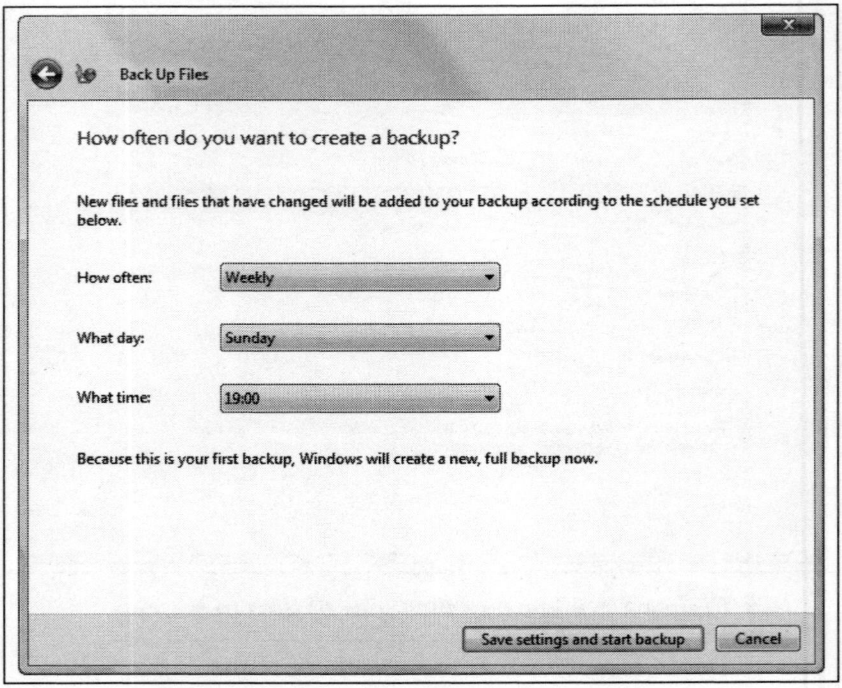

Figure 5-7 Setting the frequency of the backups

The backup will then commence – you can monitor the status as it is taking place.

Once the backup has completed successfully you should see the Backup Status and Configuration screen shown in Figure 5-8.

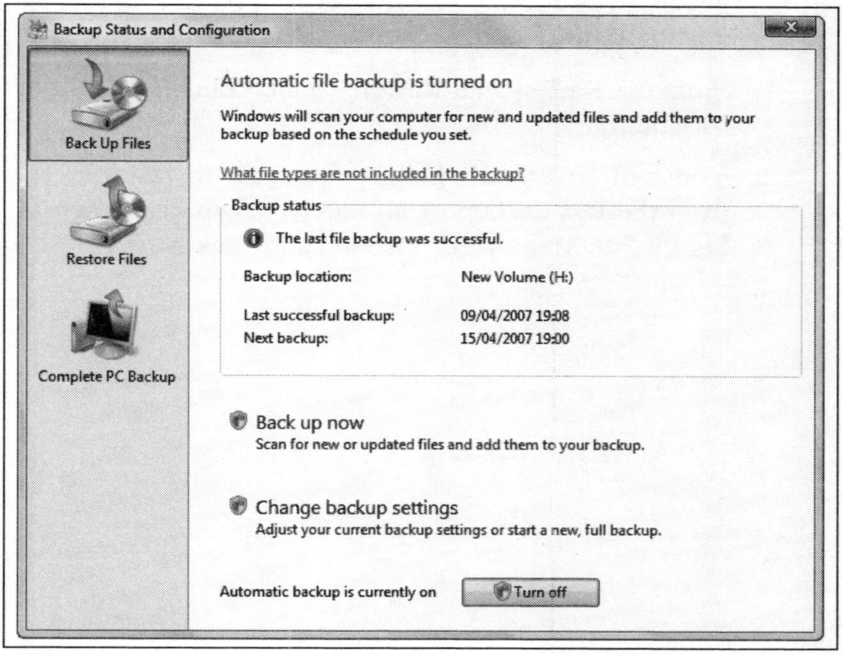

Figure 5-8 Backup Status and Configuration screen

From here you can see where and when the last backup was, and also when the next backup is due to take place. You can also choose to turn off the automatic backup if you wish.

Performing a Restore

There may come a time when you need to restore some or all of the files that you backed up previously. You can do this by performing the following steps:

1. From the Backup and Restore Center, click the Restore files button.
2. You will be asked whether you want to restore files from the last backup or an older backup, as shown in Figure 5-9. Make your selection and click Next.

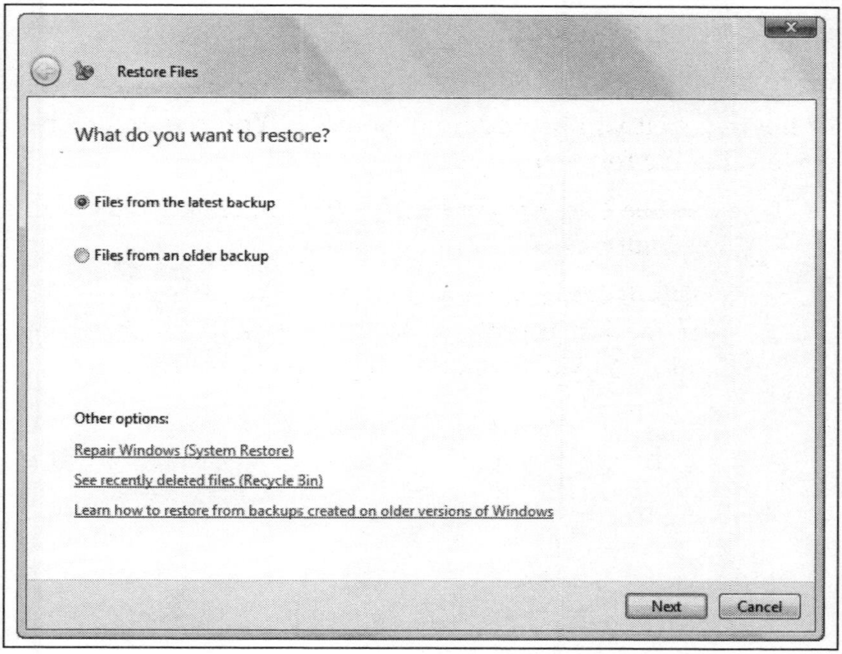

Figure 5-9 Choosing which backup to restore from

3. You will then be asked to select which files and folders you want to restore, as shown in Figure 5-10. You can then choose all the files and folders you want to restore by adding them to the list, then click on Next to continue.

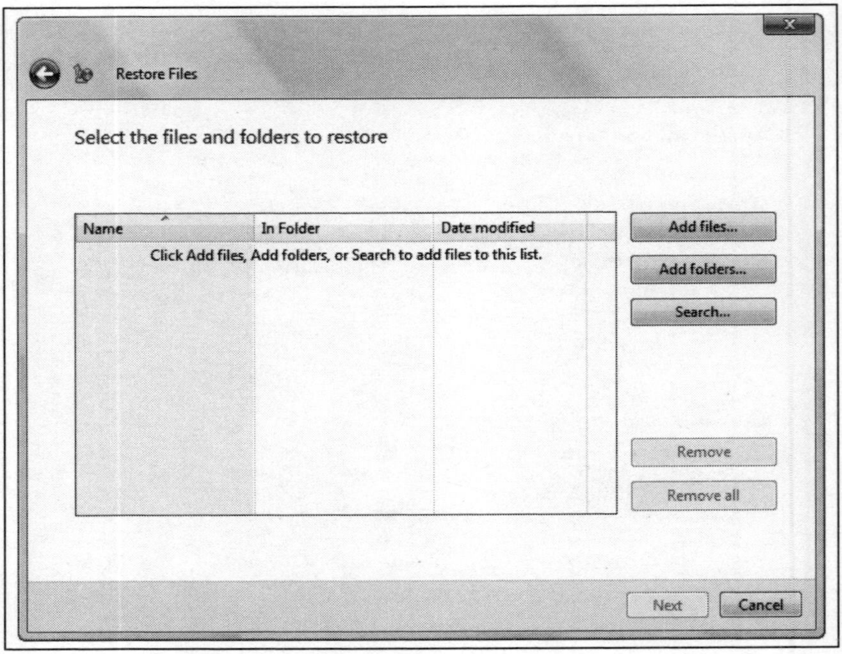

Figure 5-10 Selecting files and folders to restore

4. If you have backed up quite a lot of files, you may want a simple way of finding just one or more files. As luck would have it you can do just that by clicking on the Search button and then entering a word or words to search for, as shown in Figure 5-11 and clicking the Search button. A list will then be generated and you can select whichever files you want to add to the list by clicking on each box and then clicking the Add button.

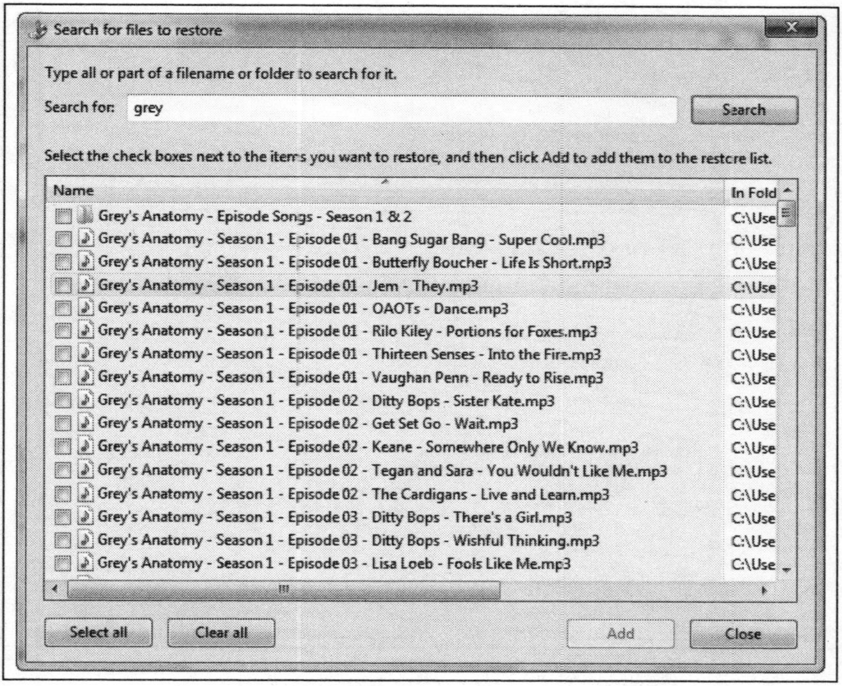

Figure 5-11 Searching for files to restore

5. You will then have the option to restore the files to their original location or to a different location, as shown in Figure 5-12. Make your location selection and then click Start Restore.

Be careful not to overwrite your existing files if you just want to restore an older version to check something!

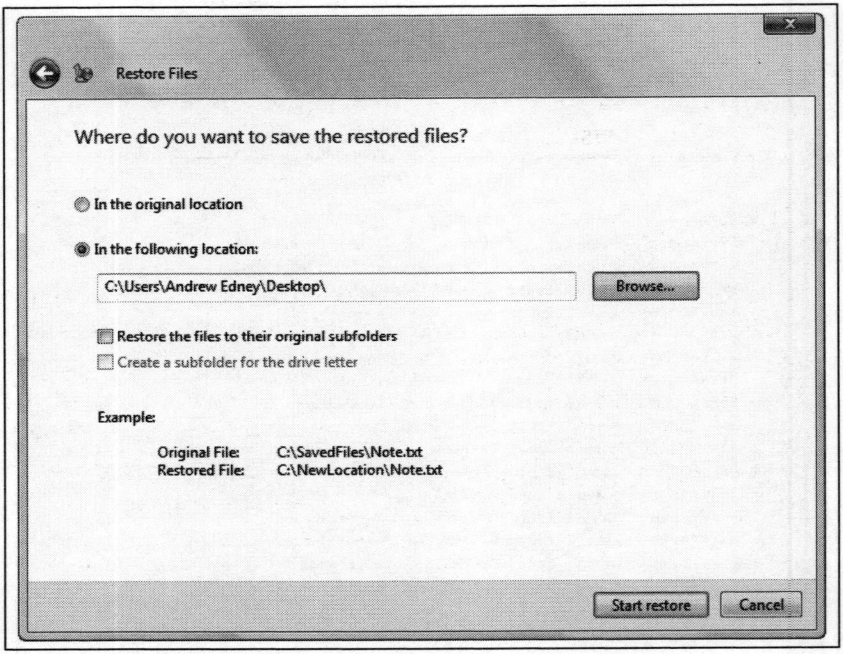

Figure 5-12 Choosing where to save the restored files

6. When the files have been restored, click Finish and then check the location you chose. If the files are not correct, or you need to go back to an earlier backup just repeat these steps and select an earlier backup, assuming that one exists.

It is a very good idea to periodically check your backups by restoring them to either a spare computer or to some free space on another drive – just to make sure they work!

Summary

So hopefully now you would have seen the uses for just a fraction of the tools that are available with Windows Vista, and that does not even include new tools that can be downloaded and installed at a later date. As with some of the other chapters, the best advice would be to have a play with each of the tools and applications to see if they are of use to you.

6

Networking

Networking is important if you want to do anything with your computer either on the Internet or on a home or office network, including connecting to other computers. You can of course quite happily use your computer "stand-alone" but then you would not benefit from all the added extras that can be gained from when you are connected either to a network, or to the Internet.

Windows Vista makes connecting to a network even easier than it has been in the past with previous versions of Windows.

Wired

To connect to a wired network is a easy as just plugging in the Ethernet cable into your computer's network card. And as long as the network card and the network you are connect to are functioning, the connection should be made and you can start being a member of the network.

Wireless

To connect to a wireless network that is in range (the network icon may flash between a disconnected network icon and some bars), perform the following steps:

1. Click on the icon.
2. On the pop-up box, as shown in Figure 6-1, click on Connect to a network.

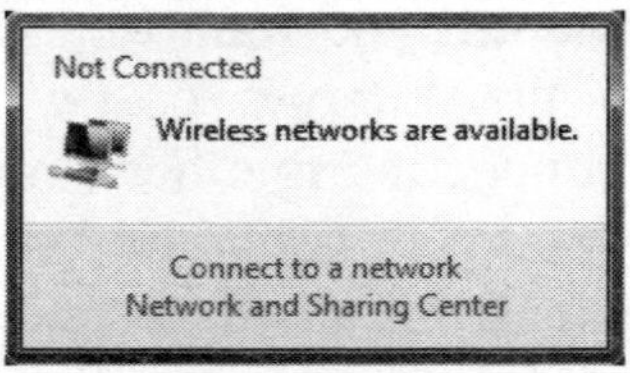

Figure 6-1 Seeing that there are wireless networks available

3. From the list of available wireless networks, as shown in Figure 6-2, click on the network you want to connect to and then click on Connect.

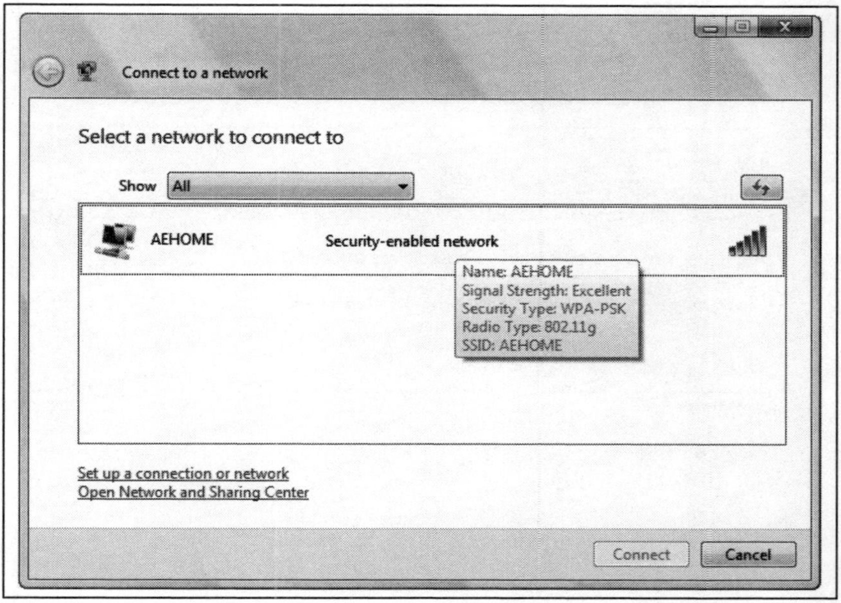

Figure 6-2 Selecting a wireless network to connect to

If you hover over one of the available networks, you will see additional information such as the signal strength, security type and radio type.

---

4. If the wireless network you are trying to connect to does not have any security associated with it, or it's a network you have previously connected to and the network security details are stored, you should now be connected to the network.

5. If the wireless network has security associated with it, you will be asked to enter the security key or passphrase to connect, as shown in Figure 6-3.

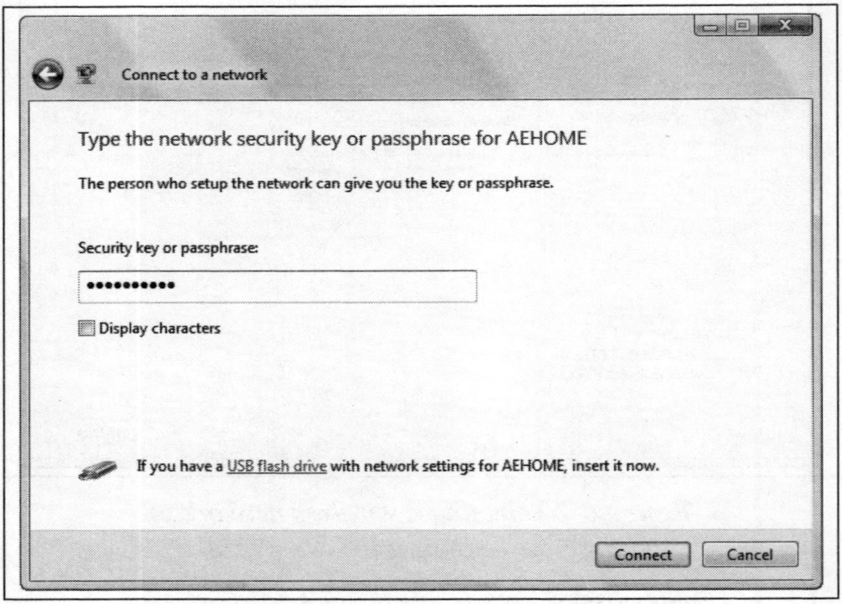

Figure 6-3 Entering your network security key or passphrase to connect to the wireless network

6. You should now be successfully connected to the network, as shown in Figure 6-4. You can choose to save the network and start the connection automatically (which is the default) so that you don't have to perform the previous steps everytime you want to connect.

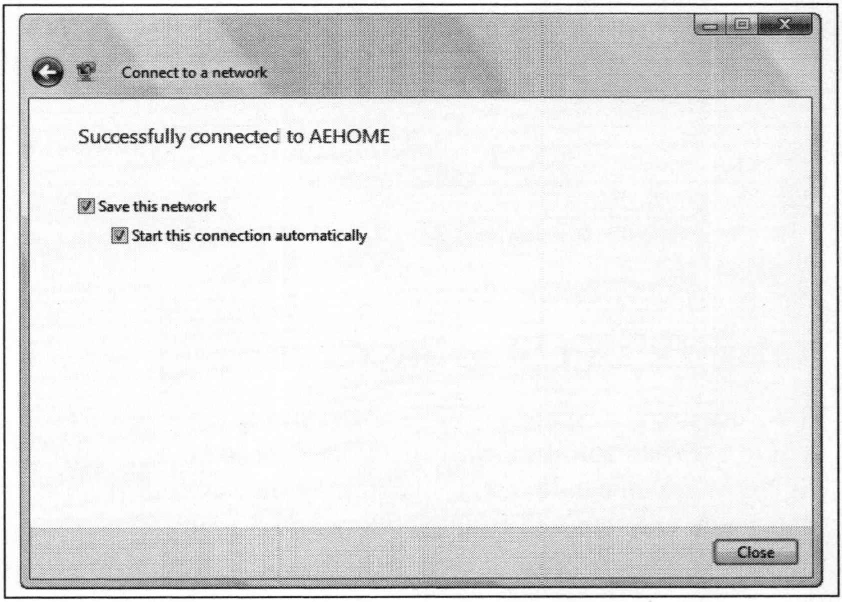

Figure 6-4 Saving the network settings and starting the connection automatically

7. Click Close to finish.

You can see information about the wireless network you are connected to at any time by either hovering over the network icon or by double-clicking the icon, as shown in Figure 6-5.

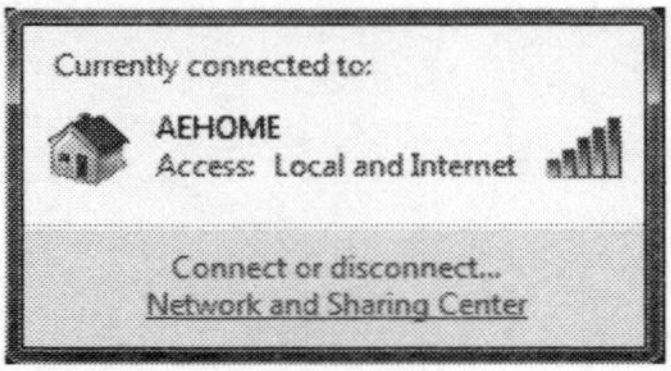

Figure 6-5 Seeing which network you are connected to

Network and Sharing Center

The Network and Sharing Center is the single place to go to in Windows Vista for all of your networking needs, as shown in Figure 6-6. You can launch it by clicking on Network from the Start menu and then selecting Network and Sharing Center.

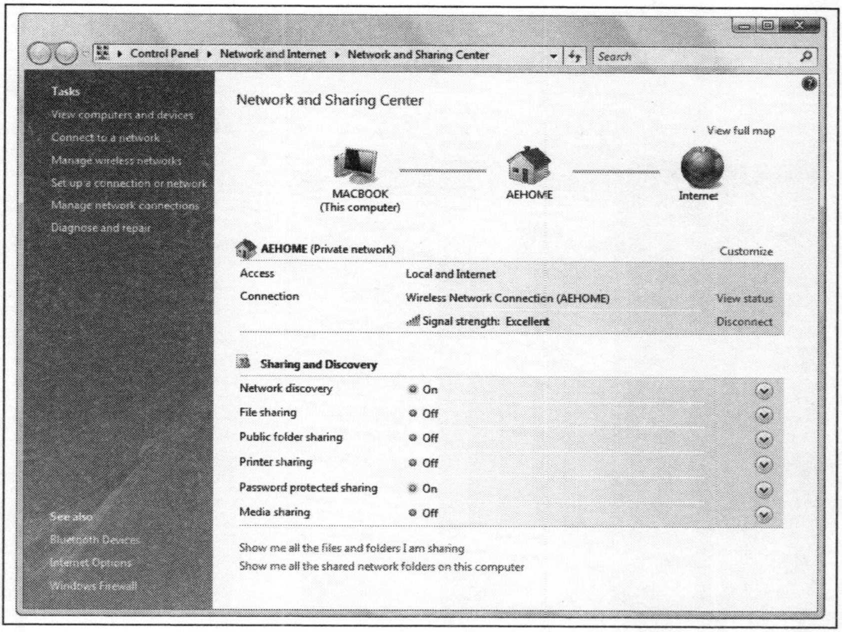

Figure 6-6 The Network and Sharing Center

From here you can check the status of your network connection, troubleshoot problems with the network, produce a picture of your network and change what you are sharing, amongst other things.

Network Map

Network Map is a new feature introduced with Windows Vista. It enables you to create a visual representation of your network, which can be useful for troubleshooting or for just seeing a single picture of your network.

You can create a network map by clicking on View Full Map in the Network and Sharing Center, as shown in Figure 6-7.

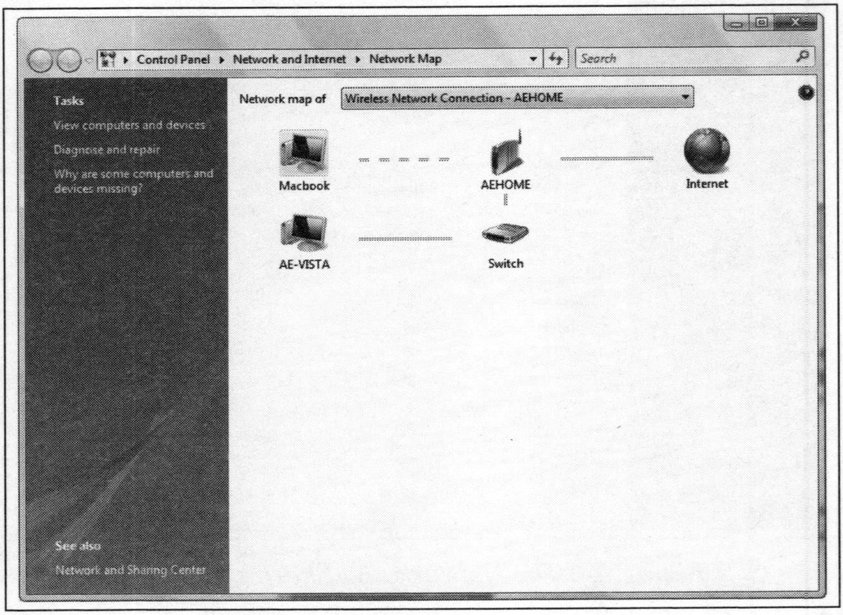

Figure 6-7 A Network Map of your network

You can then double-click on items on the map to see additional information, such as what is shared.

Customising Network Settings

You can customise your network settings at any time by clicking on Customise. You may want to change the name of your network or even change the location type, as shown in Figure 6-8.

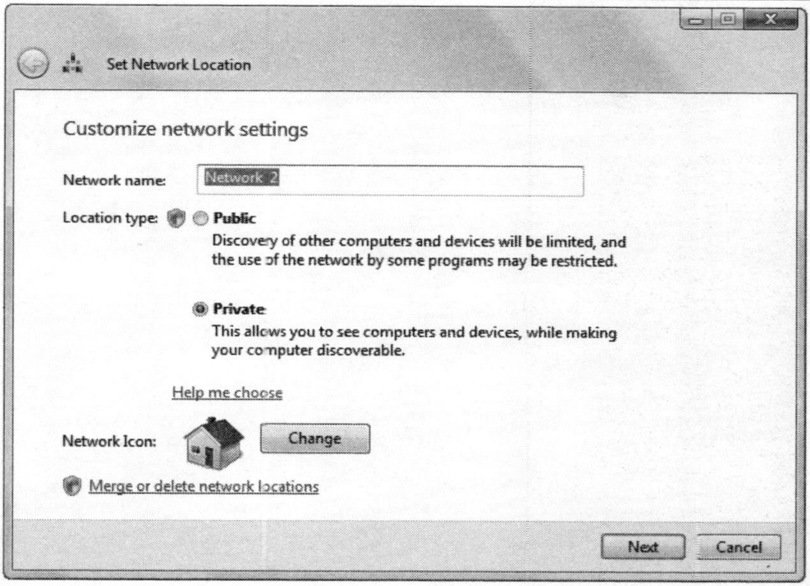

Figure 6-8 Customising network settings

If you are using your computer in a home or office environment then you will probably want to set your location type to Private.

Summary

Connecting your computer to a network has never been easier than it is now with Windows Vista, just ensure you have a working network and that you have the correct hardware, with Windows Vista drivers ready in order to connect.

7

Internet Explorer 7

Internet Explorer 7 is the latest version of Microsoft's Internet browser, and it comes bundled with Windows Vista so that you can start surfing the Internet straight away.

> You may have a preference for a different Internet browser, such as Firefox, in which case you can skip this chapter if you wish, but you may find this chapter to be useful as there are some new features in IE7 you may not know about.

This chapter will describe the new interface, how tabbed browsing works and also the built-in RSS features.

When you launch Internet Explorer you will see a screen similar to that shown in Figure 7-1.

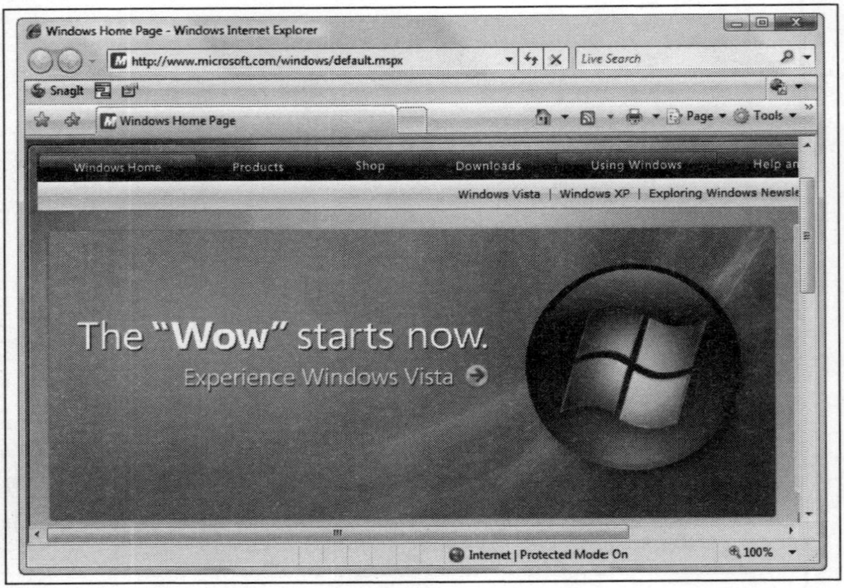

Figure 7-1 Internet Explorer 7

If you have used a previous version of Internet Explorer, the first thing you will notice is that the look and feel is completely different. Gone are the various drop-down menus, instead they have been replaced with buttons on the tool bar.

Searching the Internet

You will also notice that there is box with the words Live Search in. You can use this to search for Internet content, similar to the way you use any other search engine, for example Google. By default www.live.com is used, however if you want to use your favourite search engine you can change this.

To do so, click on the down arrow to the right of the Search box and select Find More Providers. This will bring up a list of available providers, as shown in Figure 7-2.

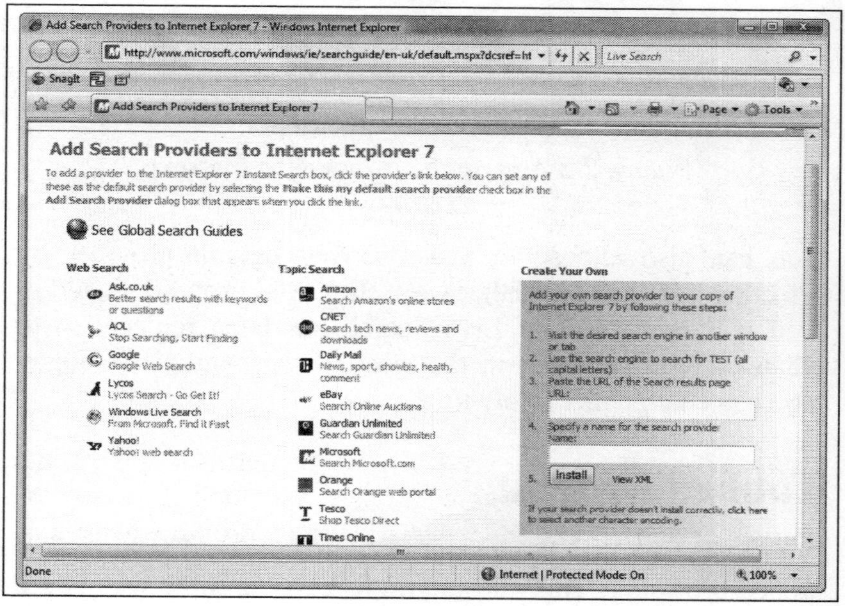

Figure 7-2 Choosing a new search provider

Click on any of the listed search providers to add them, or complete the steps to create your own. When you select an existing one, you will be asked to confirm that you want to add that search provider to Internet Explorer, as shown in Figure 7-3.

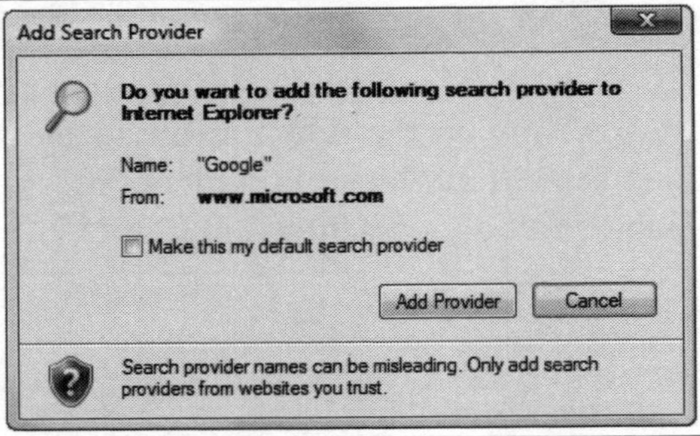

Figure 7-3 Adding the provider to Internet Explorer

You can also choose to make it your default provider by selecting the tick box. Either way, click Add Provider to add it. You will now see that Live Search has been replaced with whatever you selected, in the case of the example, Google. You can change this at any time.

Tabbed Browsing

A new feature that is introduced with Internet Explorer 7 is tabbed browsing. This allows you to have multiple web pages open in a single Internet Explorer window, each one on a separate tab.

You can easily open a new tab by clicking on the New Tab area (the small tab to the right of the last full tab) or by pressing CTRL + T, as shown on Figure 7-4.

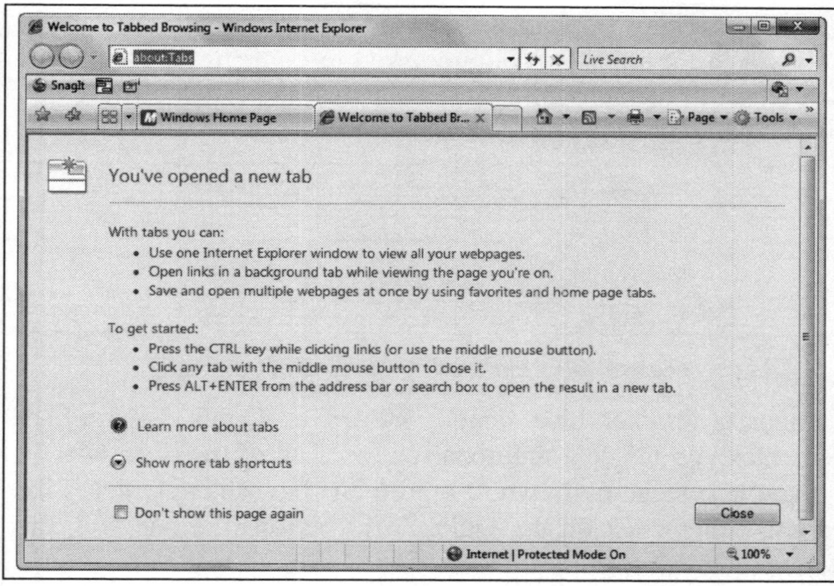

Figure 7-4 Opening a new tab

You can easily switch between the tabs by just clicking on them. You can click on links and have them either open in a new tab or in a completely new window. You can close a tab by clicking on the X to the right of each tab.

> You can easily change the order of the tabs by dragging them either left or right of their current position.

Tabbed browsing takes a little getting used to. I admit that when I first started using it I hated it, but now I find it very useful. A really useful addition is a warning should you accidently chose to close the window rather than the tab, as shown in Figure 7-5. You are asked to confirm that you want to close all of the open tabs, rather than them just closing and you losing all of the open ones.

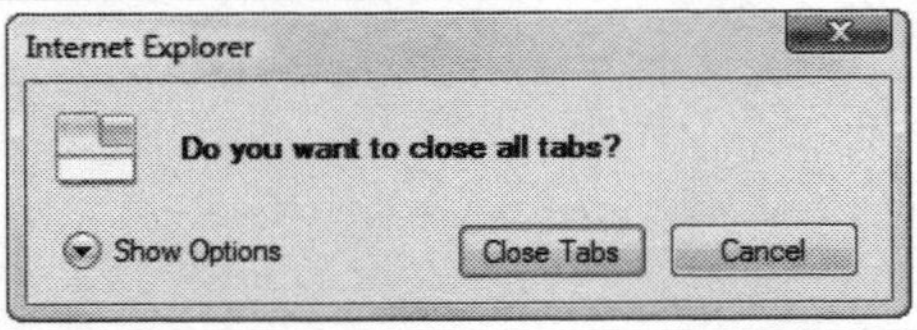

Figure 7-5 Confirming closing all the tabs

There is another nice feature known as Quick Tabs which enables you to see a thumbnail view of all of the open tabs on a single screen, as shown in Figure 7-6. To use the Quick Tabs view either click on the Quick Tabs button (the one with the four squares) or press CTRL + Q.

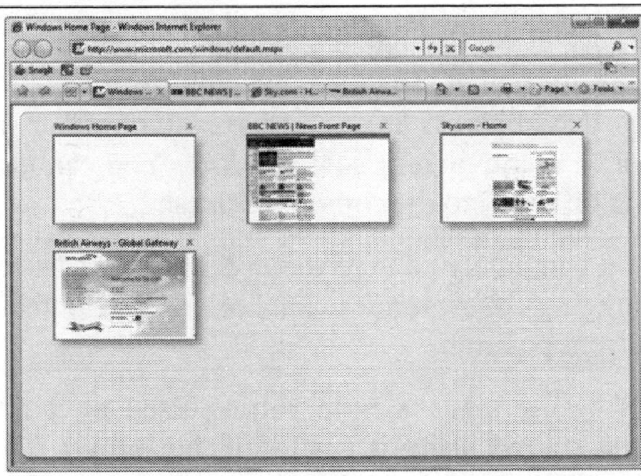

Figure 7-6 Quick Tabs view of open tabs

There are a number of settings that can be configured for tabbed browsing, including:

- Warning when closing multiple tabs
- Enabling of Quick Tabs
- How pop-ups are dealt with
- How links are dealt with

To view and change these settings do the following:

1. With an Internet Explorer window open, click on Tools.
2. Click on Internet Options.
3. Make sure you are on the General tab and click on the Settings button in the Tabs area.
4. Review and change the settings as needed, as shown on Figure 7-7.
5. Click OK to finish.

Don't worry if you make a mistake or if you want the settings to be as they were before you started making changes – just click on the Restore defaults button to put everything back to how it was.

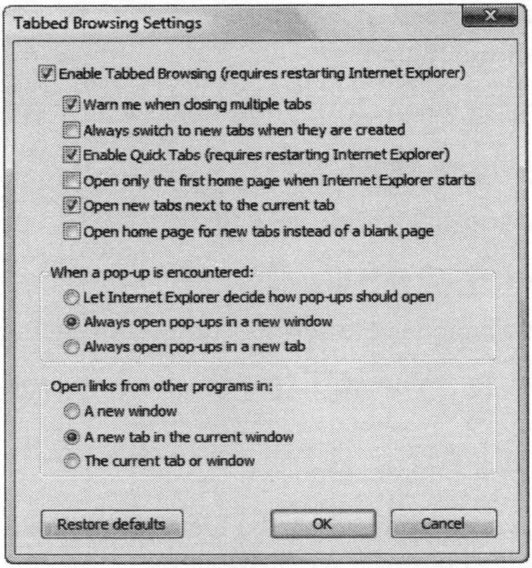

Figure 7-7 Changing tabbed browsing settings

Favourites

If you have ever used Internet Explorer before, you know that you can add webpages to your favourites list so that you can easily select them in the future instead of having to type the full URL address. Internet Explorer 7 is no different. Briefly, to add a webpage that you are currently viewing to your favourites, just click the Add to Favorites button (which is the button with the star and the plus sign) and choose Add to Favorites.

You can then enter a name (or leave the default) and choose where to create the favourite, as shown in Figure 7-8.

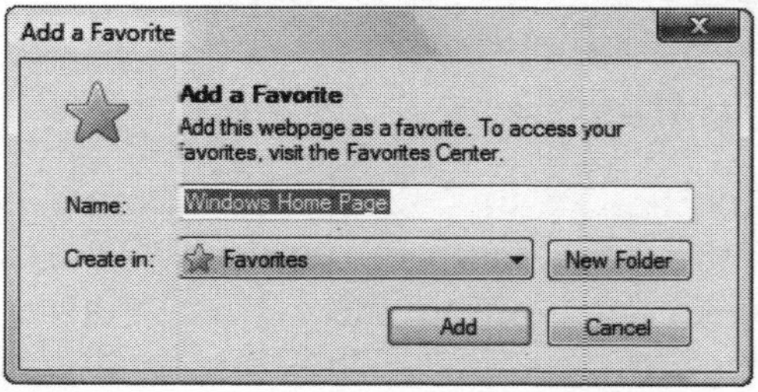

Figure 7-8 Adding a favourite webpage

Click Add when you have made any changes to add that favourite to your list. To select a favourite, just click on the Favorites button (which is the button with just the star) and select the page you want to view.

You can change the order that your favourites are displayed, or even delete favourites by clicking on the Add to Favorites button and selecting Organize Favorites.

Security Features

There are a number of security features built into Internet Explorer 7. The two primary ones are the Pop-Up Blocker, which you may already be used to with earlier versions of IE, and the Phishing Filter, which is brand new.

Even though there is a chapter devoted to security within Windows Vista (chapter 11 if you are interested), I thought it best to keep the IE security parts right here.

The Pop-Up Blocker

Anyone who has ever used the Internet would have experienced the pain that are pop-ups. These little things appear trying to sell you anything from Viagra to anti-virus products for your computer. They are really annoying and sometimes make it impossible for you to use your computer.

Also, you have no idea what else is happening when the pop-up appears. Fortunately Internet Explorer has a pop-up blocker which can be used to stop this from happening. If you use the pop-up blocker you will see a notification appear every time a pop-up is blocked, as shown on Figure 7-9 so for those rare times that the pop-up is legitimate you can allow it.

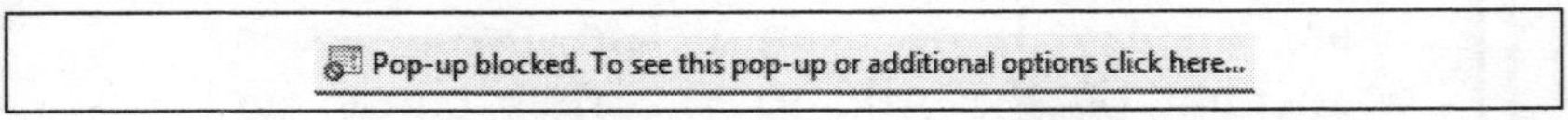

Figure 7-9 Pop-up blocked notification

By default the pop-up blocker is switched on.

Switch off the pop-up blocker at your peril!

If you visit sites that legitimately use pop-ups on a regular basis, such as your anti-virus vendor's website when looking for updates, you can add the website to an exceptions list which means whenever you visit that site, the pop-ups won't be blocked.

To add a website to the pop-up blocker exceptions list, follow these steps:

1. Click on Tools.
2. Click on Pop-up Blocker.
3. Click on Pop-up Blocker Settings – you will then see the dialog box shown in Figure 7-10.

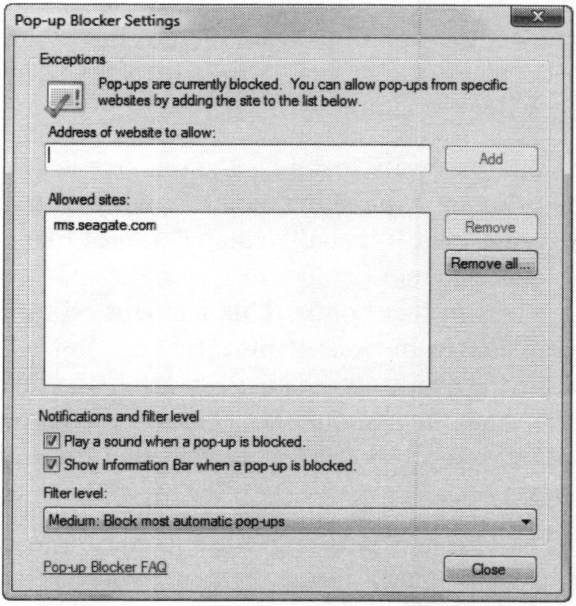

Figure 7-10 Changing the Pop-up blocker settings

4. Type in the URL of the website you want to add to the exceptions list in the Address of website to allow box.

5. Click Add to add it to the list.
6. Click Close to finish.

The filter level can be quite important. There are three settings, high, medium and low, and the default setting is medium.

- High – blocks all pop-ups
- Medium – blocks most pop-ups
- Low – allows pop-ups from secure sites

Phishing Filter

One of the other security features, and this one is new to IE7 is the Phishing Filter. A phishing attack is when you are tricked into giving your details, usually financial ones like credit card details or bank account details, to a website that you think is legitimate but is in fact bogus. This happens all the time with "alleged" emails from your bank directing you a link in an email and asking you to enter all your details so that the bank can confirm them. You should never, and I repeat never, enter your details if you are not 100% certain that the website is in fact legitimate.

This is where the phishing filter comes into play. It is designed to help detect those sorts of websites by running automatically in the background whilst you surf the Internet. It uses three methods to perform the detection:

1. It checks the URL of the site you are visiting against a list stored on your computer which is provided by Microsoft as legitimate.

2. The website is checked for common characteristics of phishing websites.
3. The URL of the website can be sent to Microsoft to check against a continually updated list of known phishing websites.

If the website you are on is designated as a phishing website, you will see a notification on the Address bar and a warning screen will be displayed.

The phishing filter is switched on by default, but it only checks the URL against the list on your computer. If you want to use any of the other checks, including the one that sends details to Microsoft you have to switch them on.

To do this, you can do the following:

1. Click on Tools.
2. Click on Phishing Filter.
3. Click on Phishing Filter settings.
4. Scroll down to the Security section and look for the Phishing Filter, as shown in Figure 7-11.
5. Make the changes you want then click on OK.

You can also manually check a website you are visiting by choosing the Check this Website option from the Tools, Phishing Filter menu.

You can also report a website that you suspect, or know, as being a phishing website by choosing the Report this Website option, also from the Tools, Phishing Filter menu.

It is a good idea to leave the Phishing Filter switched on unless you are 100% careful and always know where you are entering your personal information.

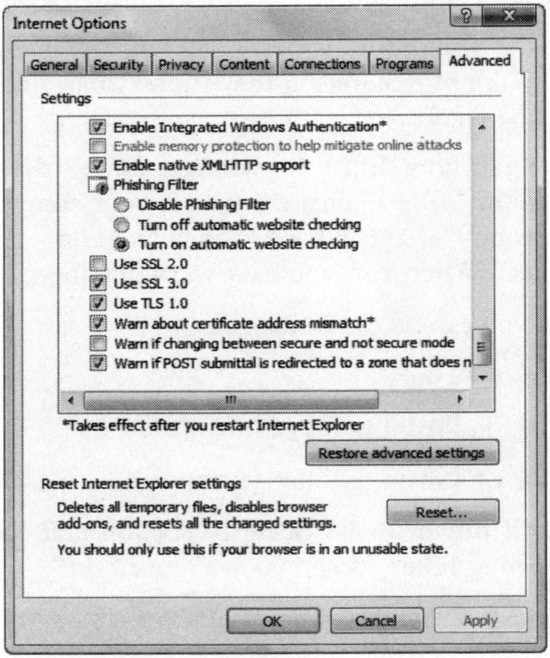

Figure 7-11 Changing the Phishing Filter settings

Protected Mode

Internet Explorer Protected Mode is a feature that makes it more difficult for malicious software to be installed on your computer without your authorisation.

> Protected Mode is switched on by default – unless you have a really good reason, leave it switched on!

You will see a warning whenever a website is trying to either install software or run an application on your computer. There may be times when this is something you actually do want to do, and so for those times you can allow it. You will see a security warning, similar to the one shown in Figure 7-12.

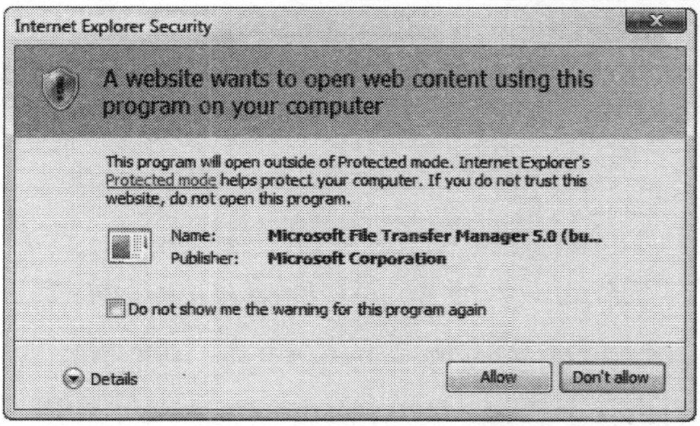

Figure 7-12 Protected Mode Warning

If you trust the provider and are happy for the application to run, just click Allow, if not, click Don't allow. You can also choose not to show the warning in the future.

RSS Feeds

RSS Feeds are something that is relatively new. RSS stands for Really Simple Syndication and is content that is frequently updated and published by websites and can be subscribed to so that you don't have to continually visit that website to see if there are any changes.

A large number of popular websites, including the BBC News website (http://news.bbc.co.uk) use RSS feeds.

> Internet Explorer 7 is not the only way to subscribe to, and read these RSS feeds. You can also use Outlook 2007 or even the RSS Feeds Headline gadget in the Sidebar.

Internet Explorer 7 will automatically check any website you visit to see if an RSS feed is available. If one is, then the RSS Feed button on the toolbar will light up, as shown in Figure 7-13.

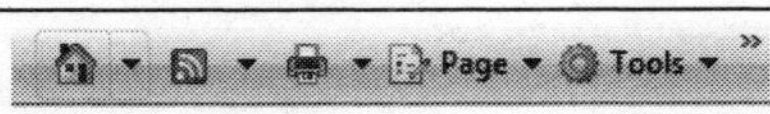

Figure 7-13 An RSS Feed is available

To subscribe to an RSS feed, perform the following steps:

1. Visit a website that you know has an RSS feed you want to subscribe to.
2. Click on the Arrow next to the RSS Feeds button (which should be lit up).
3. Select the feed you want to want from the list.

4. A webpage will appear along with an information box at the top of the page with information and a link to subscribe to the feed, as shown in Figure 7-14.
5. Click on the Subscribe to this feed link.

Figure 7-14 Option to subscribe to a feed

6. A new dialog box will appear, as shown in Figure 7-15. You can change the name of the feed and also where you want to create it.

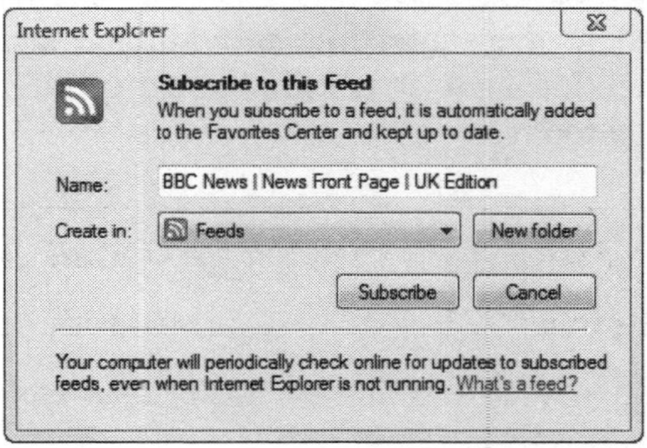

Figure 7-15 Subscribing to a feed

7. Click Subscribe to complete the steps.

You can now access that feed in a number of different ways.

The easiest way is to select it from your Favourites list. To do this, click on the Favorites button and select the Feeds button, as shown in Figure 7-16. You can then just select the feed you want to view.

Figure 7-16 Selecting a feed from Favorites

Summary

So that was a brief look at Internet Explorer 7 and some of its new features. It does take a little getting used to, but when you are used to it, you will find it to be quite user friendly and easy to use, whilst at the same time providing a welcome added layer of protection against possible security threats that exist on the Internet today.

8

Media Player 11

With the release of Windows Vista, comes the newest version of Windows Media Player – version 11.

> You can also download and install Windows Media Player 11 for Windows XP, although some of the functionality is a little different.

This chapter will give you a brief look at the new interface, the music library and more.

Configuring Media Player

The very first time you start Windows Media Player, you will be asked to configure a few options.

1. Click on Windows Media Player from the Start menu.
2. You will be asked to choose the initial settings for Media Player, as shown in Figure 8-1. Either select

Express Settings to have Media Player configure the default settings for you, or select Custom Settings to choose the options yourself. Either way, click Next when you have selected the option.

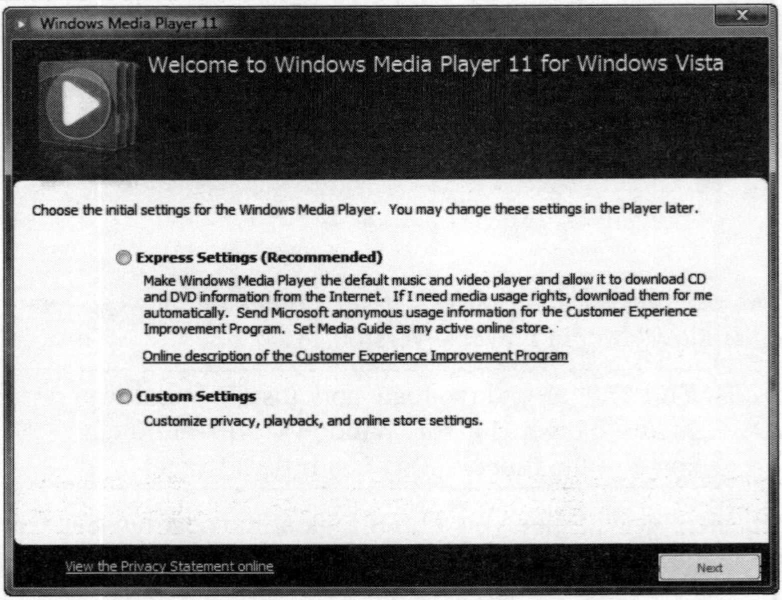

Figure 8-1 Choosing the initial settings

The rest of this walk-through assumes you selected Custom Settings.

---

3. You will then be presented with a number of different Privacy Options, as shown in Figure 8-2. Adjust any of

these privacy settings as you see fit and then click Next.

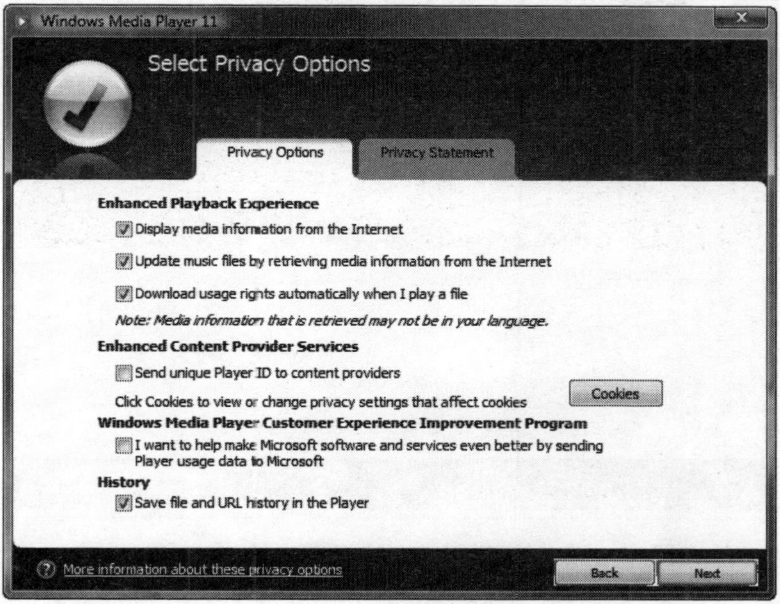

Figure 8-2 Setting Privacy Options

4. You will then have the option to Add a shortcut to the desktop and also a shortcut to the Quick Launch bar, as shown in Figure 8-3. Make your selections and click Next to continue.

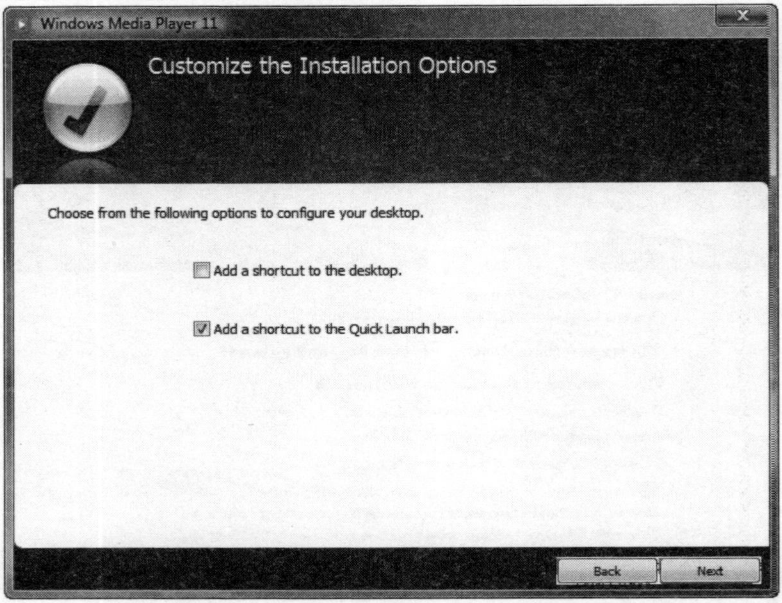

Figure 8-3 Adding shortcuts to Media Player

5. You will then be asked if you want to make Media Player 11 default music and video player – select Make Windows Media Player 11 the default music and video player, then click Next. Changing the associations will display the screen shown in Figure 8-4 and you can go through and set each media type to a certain application if you so wish.

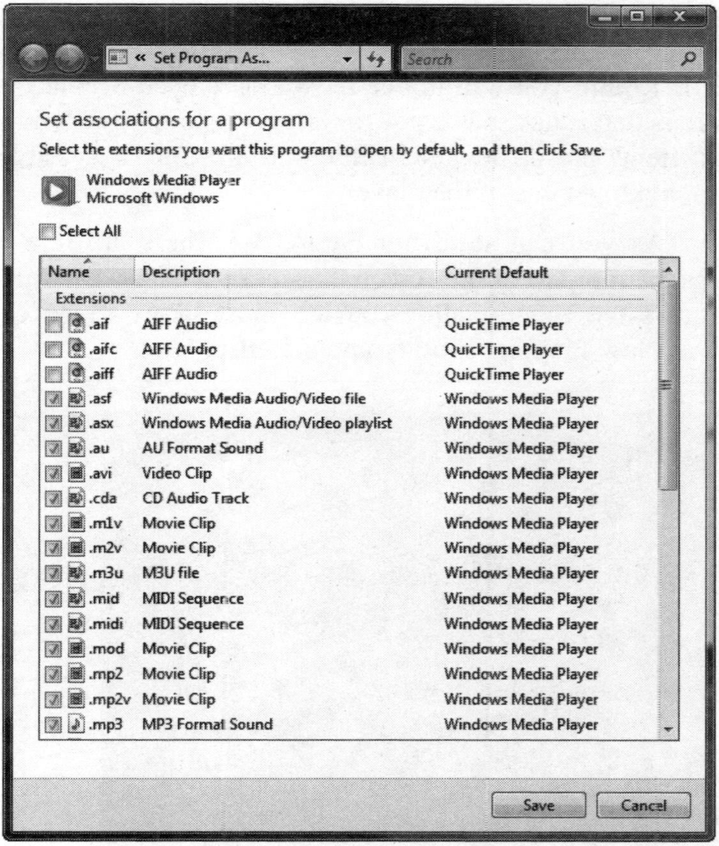

Figure 8-4 Choosing applications to play back media files

6. You then have the option of choosing an online store to use – for now just click Don't set up a store now, then click Finish.

The New Interface

The first thing you will notice if you have used Media Player before is that it now has a new interface. A lot of the "original" menu items are no longer visible and are only accessible by right-clicking areas of the player.

As you can see from Figure 8-5, there are now tabs across the top part of the screen that make it easier and quicker to access the functionality you are most likely to be using, such as Now Playing, Library and also Rip.

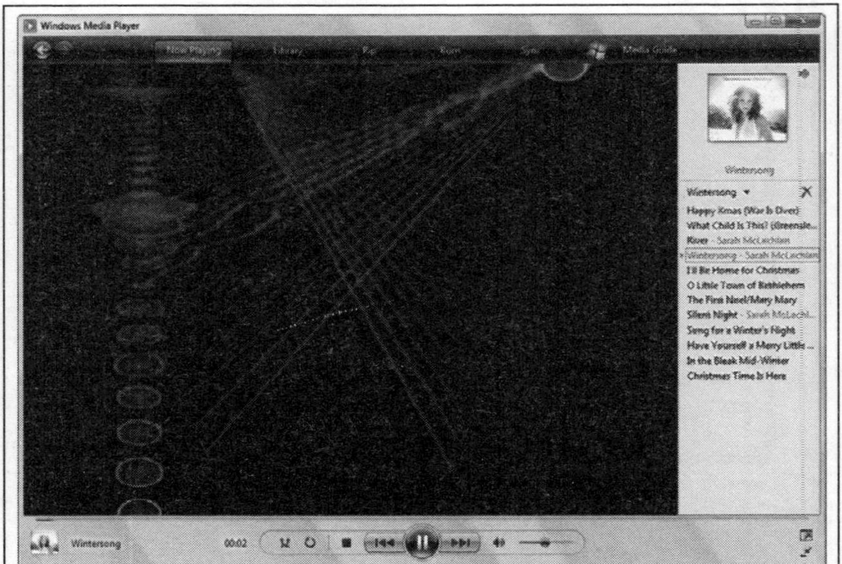

Figure 8-5 The New Interface

If you are playing music, you can choose what appears in the main window – for example, random patterns, or even the song artwork. Obviously if you are playing a video or a movie it will appear in this window.

The Library

The library is your central location for all of your music, videos and any other digital content. When you click on the Library tab you will be able to view the contents, as shown in Figure 8-6.

Figure 8-6 The Library

You can sort the views in the library in any way that makes it easier for you to find the content that you are looking for, for example you could choose just to display the albums, as shown in Figure 8-7.

Figure 8-7 Viewing the albums in the Library

You can easily play something by just selecting it and then you can control it using the buttons at the bottom of the window.

> You can also easily find content by entering something in the search box – this saves you a considerable amount of time if you happen to have hundreds or even thousands of digital files in your library.

Ripping Music to your Library

If you want to add music to your library instead of having to have the audio CD in your computer it is very simple.

1. Ensure the audio CD you want to copy is in the computer.
2. Click on the Rip tab.
3. The song list and album artwork should then appear, as shown in Figure 8-8. You can choose to rip the entire CD or just certain tracks. Either way, click on Start Rip to begin.

Figure 8-8 Deciding which songs to rip

You will need to be connected to the Internet in order to retrieve the song list and the album artwork.

---

4. The Rip Options screen will then appear, as shown in Figure 8-9. You must decide whether or not to add copy protection to your music, and then tick the I understand that music copied from CDs is protected by law button, then click OK.

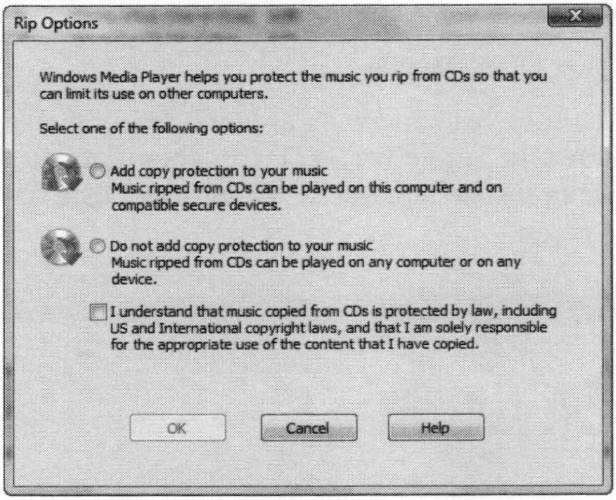

Figure 8-9 Choosing the Rip options

5. The CD will then begin to be ripped. You can monitor the progress as shown in Figure 8-10. At any time you can stop the rip by clicking on the Stop Rip button.

Figure 8-10 Monitoring the progress of the rip

Changing the Rip Options

You can change the default settings that Media Player uses to rip your music by clicking on the down arrow at the bottom of the Rip tab and selecting More Options and selecting the Rip Music tab. This will display the Options screen, as shown in Figure 8-11.

From here you can change the location of where your music is stored on your computer.

You can also change the format of the ripped songs. By default the setting is Windows Media Audio (WMA) but you can set it to any other available option, such as MP3. You can also choose to automatically Rip a CD when it is inserted and also change the audio quality.

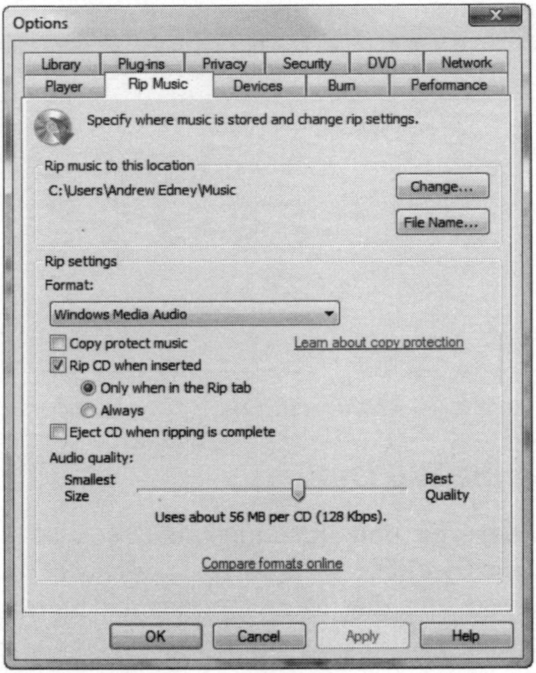

Figure 8-11 Changing the Rip options

Remember that the better the quality of the audio, the more disc space is used, so make sure you find the right balance. For most people 128 Kbps is sufficient unless you really want something better.

Playlists

You can easily create any number of playlists which makes listening to your favourite music even simpler. You can create playlists to match your mood, the day of the week, or anything you like. Then when you want to listen to the music in the playlist, all you have to do is select the playlist to begin playing all the music you have previously selected.

To create a playlist, do the following:

1. Ensure you are in the Library, as shown in Figure 8-12.

Figure 8-12 Creating a playlist

2. Click on the Create Playlist button from the Playlists list.

3. Enter a name for the playlist, in the case of Figure 8-12, I have called the playlist Andrews Music.
4. Now just drag music from your library onto the area marked "Drag items here".
5. When you are happy with the songs in the playlist just click on Save Playlist.
6. Click on your new playlist to start listening to it.

Burning Music CDs

You might decide that you want to create a music CD of your favourite music. You do this by performing the following steps:

1. Click on the Burn tab, as shown in Figure 8-13.
2. Choose the music you want to burn to CD and just drag it to the burn list, in a similar way to what you did to create a playlist.
3. You can change the order of the music into whichever order you want to.

> You can also easily burn an audio CD of any playlist by selecting the playlist before you clicked on Burn and then clicking on the Burn 'playlist' link.

4. When you have added all of the music to the Burn List, click on the Start Burn button.

Figure 8-13 Burning a music CD

5. Insert a blank CD into your computer and Windows will automatically detect it and start the burn, as shown in Figure 8-14.

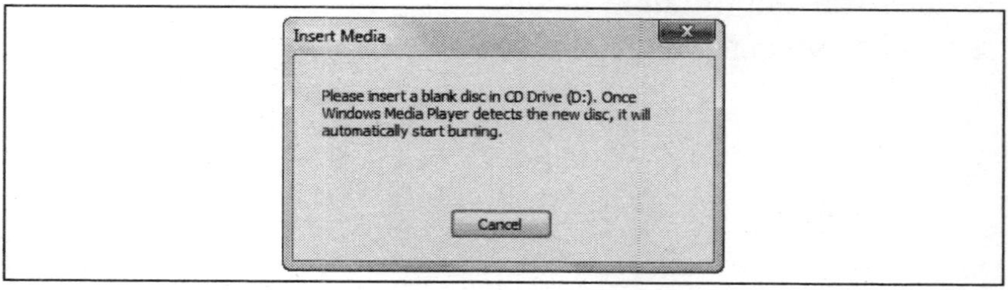

Figure 8-14 Insert a blank CD

6. You can then monitor the progress of the burning, as shown in Figure 8-15.

Figure 8-15 Monitoring the burn process

Sync

The sync function enables you to synchronise media files between your computer and portable media players, such as the new Microsoft Zune device. If you connect a supported device you can drag the media files you want to the sync list and when you are happy click on Start Sync.

Media Guide

The Media Guide tab enables you to connect to a host of new and exciting media content ranging from songs to movie files, as shown in Figure 8-16.

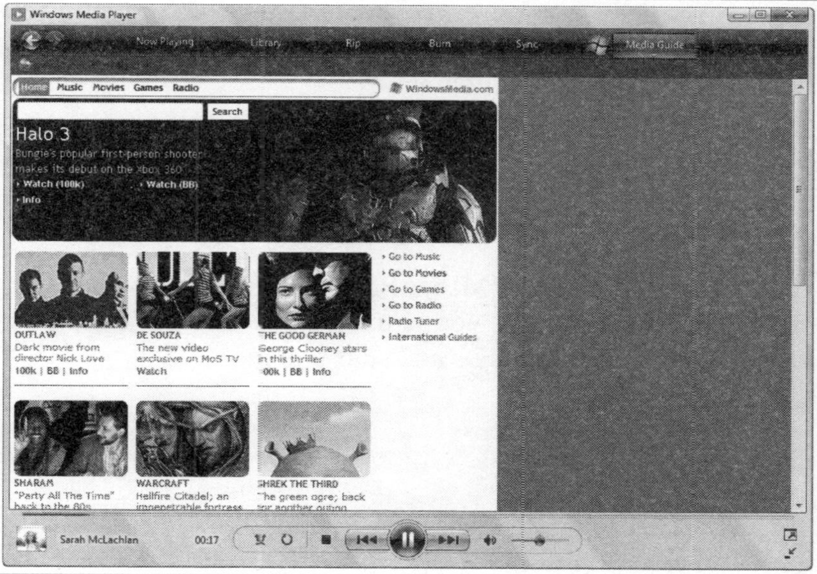

Figure 8-16 Media Guide

The Mini Player

A really nice new feature is the Mini Player. What this does is effectively shrink the Media Player down to just the controls and have it reside on the task bar, as shown in Figure 8-17.

Figure 8-17 The Mini Player

You can control your music from the mini player in the same way as you would from the main Media Player. However you now do not need to swap between whatever other program you were using and Media Player in order to change tracks, stop, pause, start or adjust the volume.

Summary

So very briefly that was Media Player 11. The best way to see what it can really do for you is to experiment with it. So grab some of your favourite CDs and start playing!

9

Vista Media

Apart from Media Player 11 which you now know all about, and Windows Media Center, which you will learn all about in the next chapter, Vista has a number of other applications as part of the operating system that help you to create, edit and manipulate different sorts of media content. This chapter will introduce you to the Windows Movie Maker, Photo Gallery and DVD Maker, all of which can be very useful in helping you to let your creative juices flow.

Windows Movie Maker

Windows Movie Maker is a great tool which has been designed to help you to import, edit and manage your digital home movies. You can import movies directly from your video camera if you want to, and it even supports High Definition (HD) video for superior quality.

You can also import pictures and music to use in your movie creation.

You can launch Windows Movie Maker by selecting it from the Program Files menu.

The first thing you will need to do is import some media content to use in your movie.

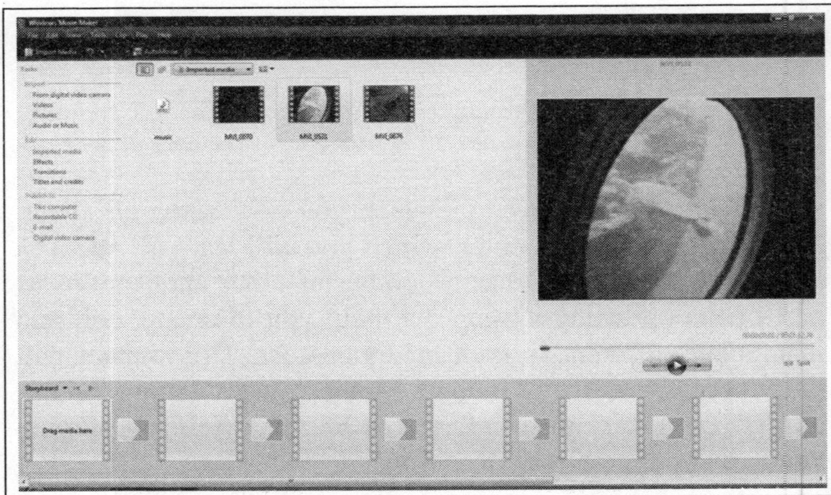

Figure 9-1 Windows Movie Maker

You can do this a number of different ways, for example if you want to import a video you can click on Videos from the Import menu, or if you click on Import Media from the menu bar you can select from any type of media content. If you have a video camera connected to your computer you can import a movie directly from that camera by selecting From digital video camera from the Import menu.

Once you have imported some media files, you should see a screen similar to that shown in Figure 9-1.

Before you start putting the videos, pictures and music into some sort of order, it might be an idea to create a title and animate it. This is very simple to do, so follow these steps:

1. Click on Titles and Credits from the Edit menu list.
2. Choose where you want to add the title, for example at the beginning of the movie.
3. Type in some text that you want to appear as the title, for example "Andrew's Holiday Video". You will see a preview on the right-hand window.
4. If you want to change the animation click on Change the title animations from the More options list.
5. You can now scroll through the list of available animations, as shown in Figure 9-2 and choose one that suits you.

    Don't forget that you can see a preview of each selected animation, which is better than waiting until the end of the movie-making process only to find that you don't really like the animation after all.

6. You can also change the font and the colour of the text used by clicking on Change the text font and colour from the More options list.

7. When you have made all the selections you want and you are happy, click Add Title to finish.

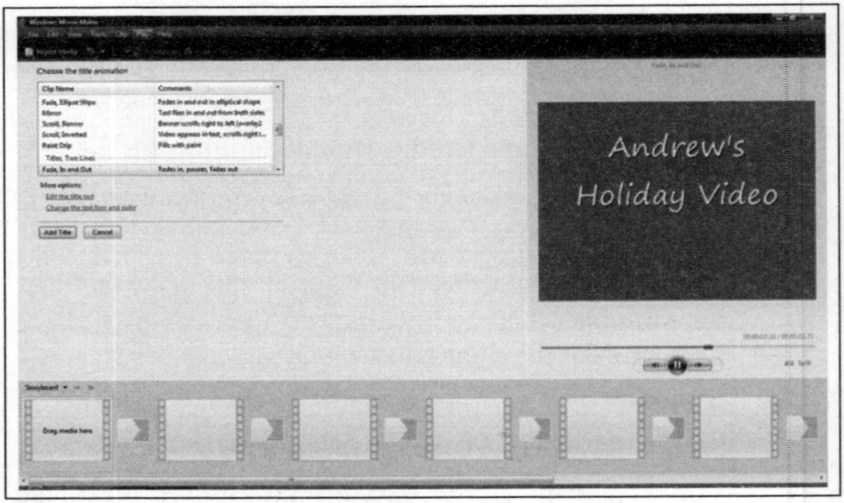

Figure 9-2 Choosing a title animation

The next step is to add the media content you imported earlier and place it on the storyboard in the sequence you want to display it. To do this, just drag the media files to the relevant empty squares on the storyboard.

Once you have added your media content onto the storyboard you might want to add some transitions to make the change between the different movies look better and create a more enjoyable viewing experience.

1. Click on Transitions from the Edit menu list. Figure 9-3 shows some of the various transitions that can be selected.

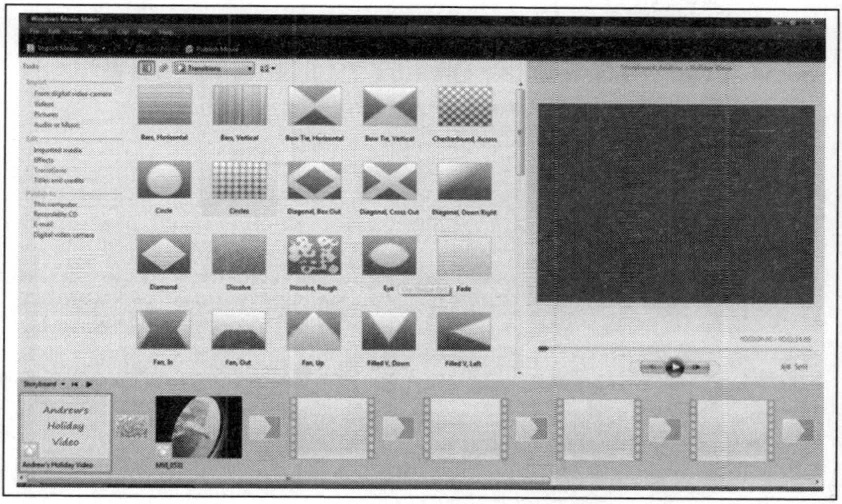

Figure 9-3 Selecting transitions

2. If you want to see what each transition will look like, click on it and then click the Play button under the preview window.
3. When you have decided on a transition, just drag it to the relevant empty transition box on the storyboard between the media clips.
4. Repeat this process for each transition you want to add to your storyboard.

You can also add some effects to your movie, for example you can "age" the film to make it look like it was shot many years ago on an old camera.

There are many different effects that can be effectively used to enhance your movie – have a play around with them to see which better suits your movie.

1. Click on Effects from the Edit menu list. Figure 9-4 shows some of the various effects that can be selected.

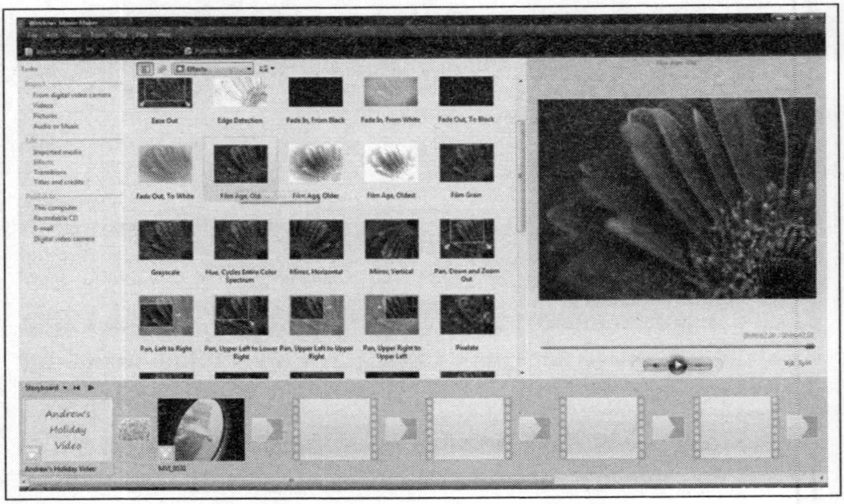

Figure 9-4 Choosing an effect

2. If you want to see what each effect will look like, click on it and then click the Play button under the preview window.
3. When you have decided on an effect, just drag it to the relevant movie clip box on the storyboard in order to apply that effect to that specific clip.

4. Repeat this process for each effect you want to add to your clips on the storyboard.

You can also add music or other sounds to your movie.

1. From the Imported Media screen, select the music and drag it to a place on your storyboard. The view will automatically be changed to a Timeline view, as shown in Figure 9-5.

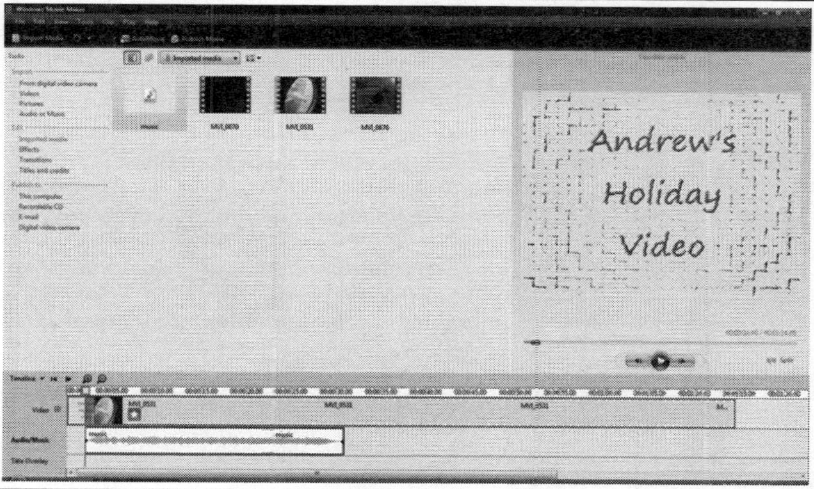

Figure 9-5 Adding music to the timeline

2. You can then drag the music clip on the timeline to any position you want. You can even shorten the clip, but if you are going to do that, you might want to consider trimming the end of the clip otherwise it might sound a little strange.

3. Repeat the steps to add as much music or sound as you want.

And don't forget that you can preview your entire movie at any time by clicking on the Play button under the preview window.

Finally, before you publish the movie, why not add a set of credits, as shown in Figure 9-6. To do this, it is exactly the same as before when you added titles.

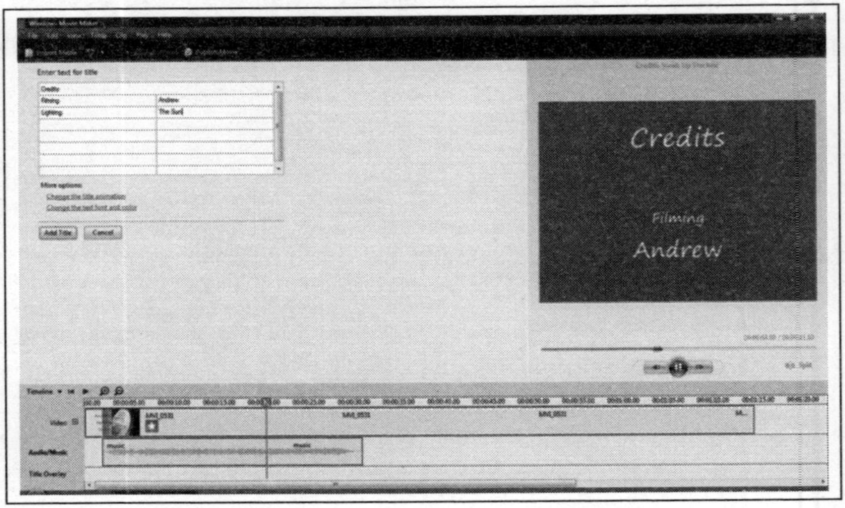

Figure 9-6 Adding some credits to your movie

When you have completely finished adding movies, sounds, transitions, effects and anything else you want to do, it is time to publish your finished masterpiece. You have four options available for publishing, as shown in Figure 9-7:

- This computer (so you can play it back straight away on your computer)
- DVD (so you can play it back on your DVD player)
- Recordable CD (so that you can play it back on any computer or device that supports the playback of WMV files)
- Email (so that you can email it to someone else)
- Digital video camera (so that you can record it onto a digital video tape)

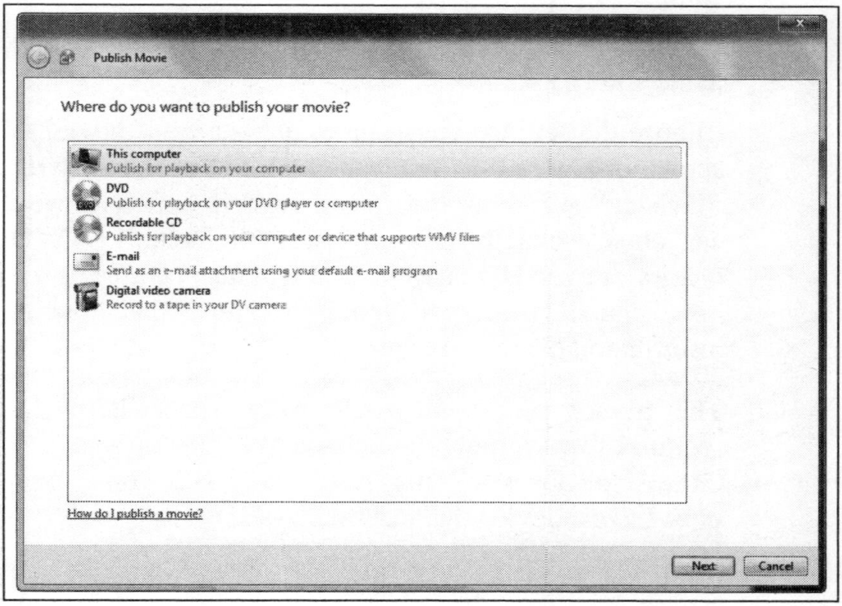

Figure 9-7 Publishing options

If you choose to publish your movie to DVD, Windows Movie Maker will close and Windows DVD Maker will open.

To publish your movie, follow these steps (these steps are for publishing to a Recordable CD, although the steps are similar for other locations):

1. Choose where you want to publish your movie from the Publish to menu.
2. Ensure you have a blank recordable CD in your computer.
3. Name the movie you are publishing, including a File name and CD name.
4. Choose the settings you want to use for your movie, as shown in Figure 9-8. You can choose "Best Quality for Playback" which is the recommended option or you can choose exactly how you want it including DVD quality or even HD quality. You will also be able to see how much space is required and other useful information displayed here.

The higher the quality, the more space is required so you might not be able to fit this on a CD. Also, don't forget if you select HD you must have a device that can display HD!

5. Click on Publish to begin the movie creation and writing process.

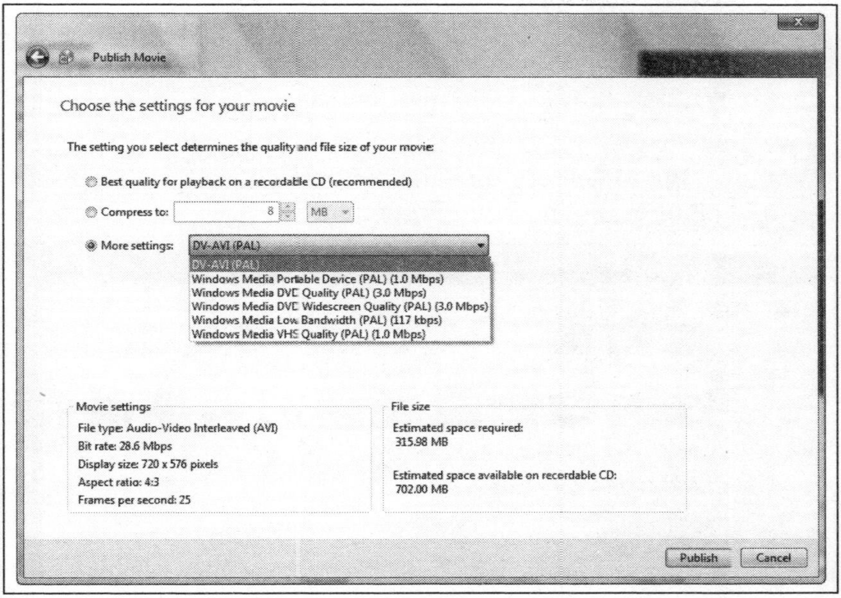

Figure 9-8 Choosing your movie settings

6. When the creation and writing has completed, you will be given the option to create another CD or finish.

Windows Photo Gallery

Windows Photo Gallery is a great tool for viewing and manipulating both your photos and videos (yes, I did say videos). You can create slide shows, change the orientation of the pictures, add tags and captions, do basic photo editing and various other things including printing your pictures.

To launch Windows Photo Gallery, just select it from the Program Files list.

The first thing you will see are any pictures that are in your current gallery. If this is the first time you have started Windows Photo Gallery then the pictures you see are the usual sample pictures, as shown in Figure 9-9.

Figure 9-9 Viewing pictures in the Gallery

Adding Your Pictures to the Gallery

To add a folder of your own pictures to the gallery, perform the following steps:

1. Click on File on the top bar.
2. Click on Add to Gallery.
3. Select the folder you want to add then click OK.

4. You should then see a message telling you that the folder has been added to the gallery, as shown in Figure 9-10.

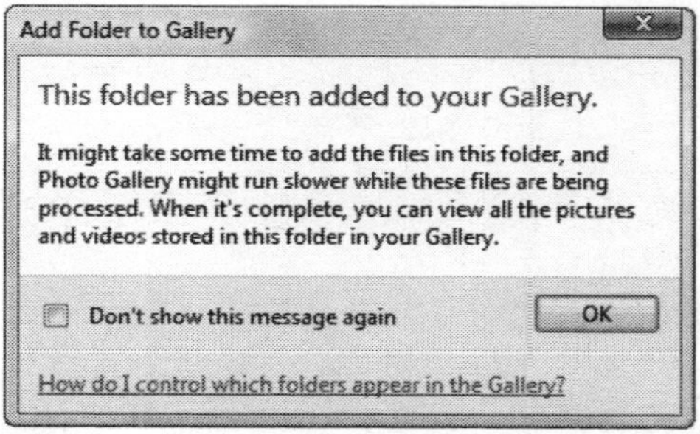

Figure 9-10 Confirmation that the folder of pictures has been added to the gallery

5. Click OK to finish.

You can also choose to import pictures directly from your digital camera or from a scanner if you so wish.

You will then be able to see your pictures displayed in the gallery, as shown in Figure 9-11.

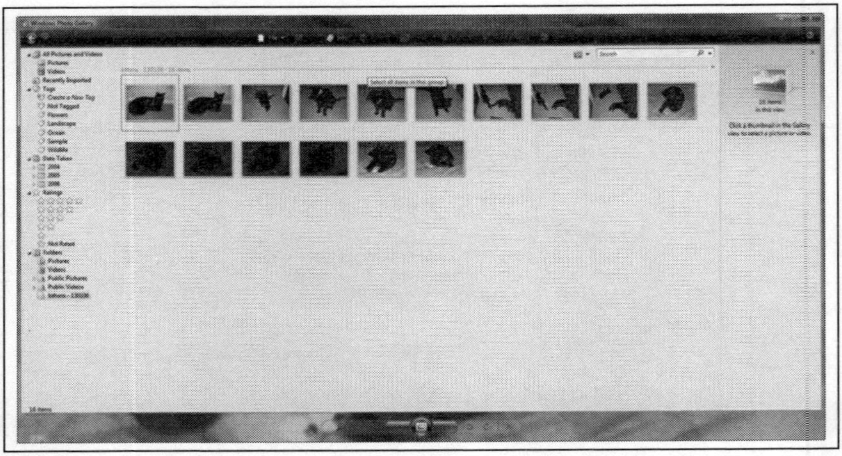

Figure 9-11 Your pictures in the gallery

If you hover the mouse pointer over a specific picture, it will appear larger and you will be able to see any additional information, such as the date and time the picture was taken, along with a rating and any tags you have added, as shown in Figure 9-12.

You can assign a rating from 0 stars to 5 stars depending on how much you like the picture. You can then easily search for pictures later by specifying only pictures with a certain number of stars.

Figure 9-12 Examining a picture in more detail

Fixing Your Pictures

You might find that you want to make some minor adjustments to one or more of your pictures in order to make it a little bit better.

To do this, all you have to do is select a picture and then click on Fix from the menu bar. This will open the picture and present you with a number of options, as shown in Figure 9-13.

These options include:

- Auto adjust (which will correct the exposure and colour of picture for you).
- Manual exposure and colour adjust (for making manual changes when auto adjust just will not do).
- Crop picture

- Fix Red Eye

Figure 9-13 Fixing your picture

Windows Photo Gallery only offers very basic options for photo editing – if you want to do anything more than the few options provided you should consider buying a more professional package such as Adobe Photoshop.

Online Printing

If you don't have a colour printer, of if you want to have your pictures printed professionally, you don't have to take them into your local shop on a memory card anymore. Windows Photo Gallery has the ability to find a store in your area that will be able to print your pictures for you over the Internet.

To use this feature, perform the following steps:

1. Select the pictures you want printed
2. Click on Print then select Order Prints. Windows Photo Gallery will automatically find any companies in your area that will perform this service.

   Don't forget you will need to be connected to the Internet to use this service.

3. Select the printing company you want to use, as shown in Figure 9-14 and then click Send Pictures.
4. You will be warned that sending pictures over the Internet may contain personal information. Click Send to send the pictures if you are happy to do so.

   Depending on the speed of your Internet connection and the number and size of the pictures you want to send, this process may take a little time – so be patient.

5. Follow the on-screen prompts and requests for information from the printing company until your order is complete.

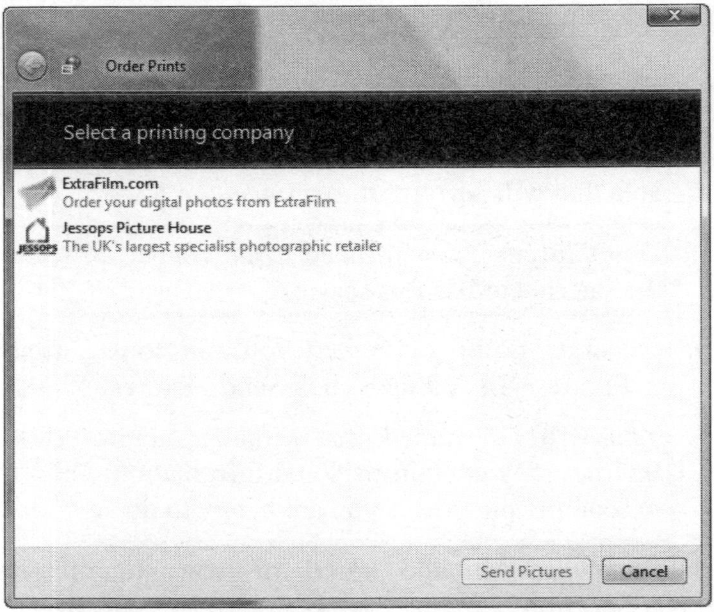

Figure 9-14 Selecting the online printing company

Printing Your Pictures Yourself

You don't have to send your pictures off to be printed professionally – you can print them yourself.

To do this, just select the picture or pictures you want to print and then click on Print from the menu bar and then select Print. This will bring up the Print Pictures dialog box, as shown in Figure 9-15.

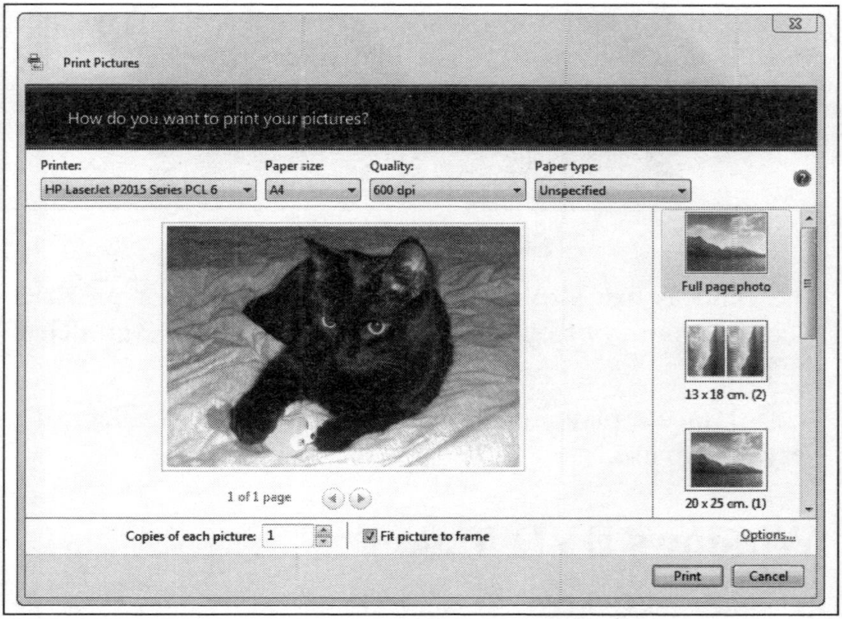

Figure 9-15 Printing your pictures

From here you can select the printer you want to print to, the paper size and type, quality of the image, how many copies you want and the types of print, such as Full page photo or even a contact sheet of all of your pictures.

When you have made your selections just click Print to start the printing going.

Slide Shows

If you want to view your pictures in a slide show, it's very easy. All you have to do is select the pictures you want to include in the slide show and then just click the Play Slide Show button or press F11. The Play Slide Show button is the centre button of the controls, as shown in Figure 9-16.

Figure 9-16 Controls

The controls can also be used to go to the next or previous picture, zoom in or out of the picture, rotate and even delete the picture.

Have a play around with Windows Photo Gallery, it's very easy to use.

Windows DVD Maker

Windows DVD Maker is very similar to Windows Movie Maker but it provides simpler functionality – essentially making it easier and quicker to create a DVD by removing some of the added functionality that Windows Movie Maker provides.

> DVD Maker is only available with Vista Home Premium edition or Vista Ultimate edition.

When you first start Windows DVD Maker, you will see the screen shown in Figure 9-17. If you never want to see that screen again just ensure there is a tick in the Don't show this page again box. Click the Choose Photos and Videos button to continue.

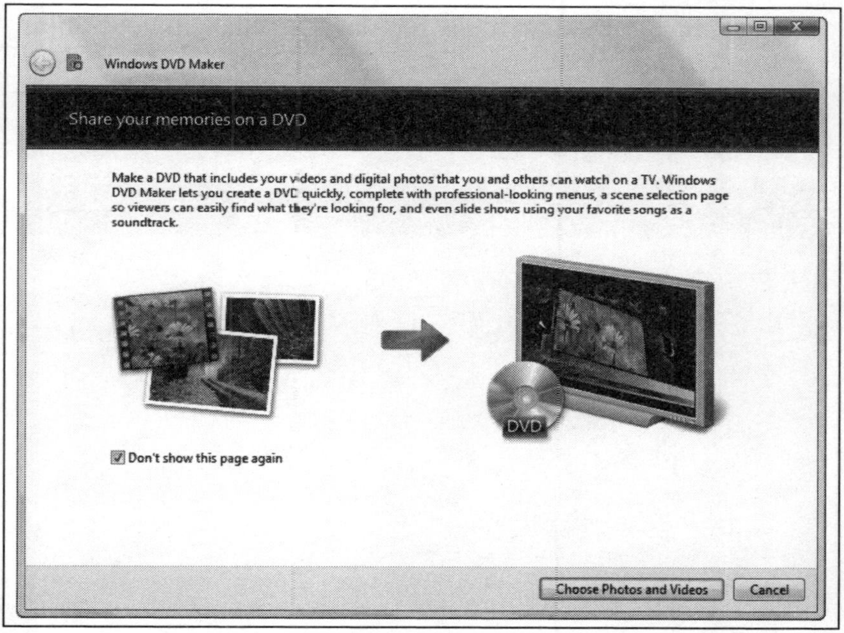

Figure 9-17 Windows DVD Maker launch screen

You will then see the Add pictures and videos to the DVD screen, as shown in Figure 9-18.

To add pictures and videos, click on the Add items button and then select whatever files you want to add to the DVD, as shown in Figure 9-19.

You can change the sequence of the items on the DVD and remove anything you later decide you don't want on there. Make sure you set the sequence correctly as once you have written the DVD it will be too late to change your mind without writing a whole new DVD.

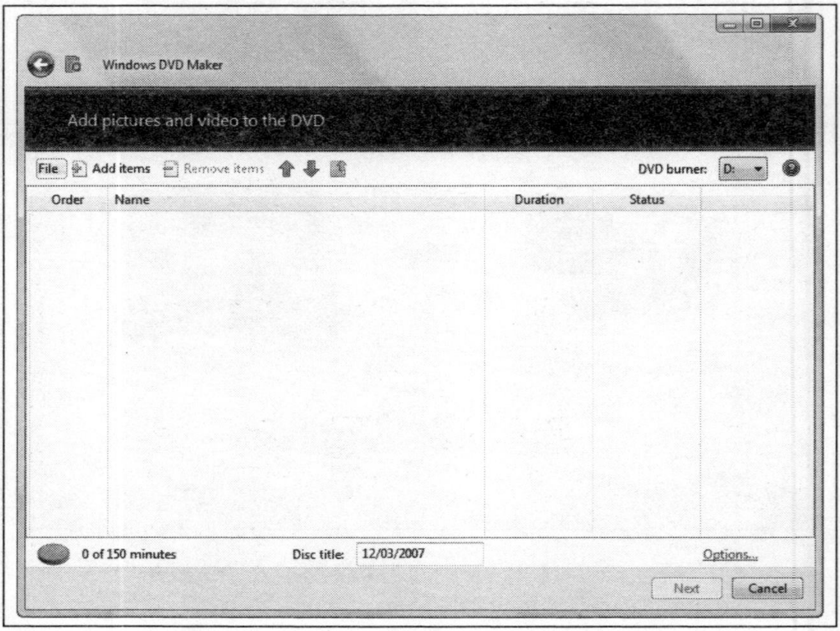

Figure 9-18 Preparing to add pictures and videos

You must ensure that the DVD burner is selected correctly, in the case of the example it is the D drive.

You can also change the title of the DVD to be something more memorable than just the date (which is the default).

You can also see how much time you have remaining on the DVD by the counter at the bottom left of the screen.

Figure 9-19 Adding your pictures and videos

If you click the Options button you will see the screen displayed in Figure 9-20.

From here you can select the DVD playback settings:

- Start with DVD menu
- Play video and end with DVD menu
- Play video in a continuous loop

To make your DVD look more professional, choose the Start with DVD menu option – which is also the default option.

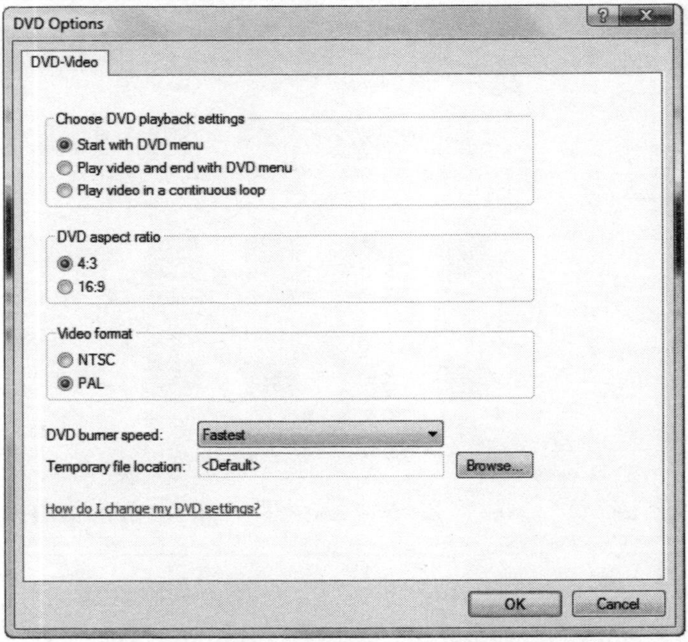

Figure 9-20 The DVD Options screen

You can also change the DVD aspect ratio. If you intend to play the DVD on a widescreen TV you should select 16:9 as the aspect ratio.

The default setting is 4:3 which may make your pictures and videos look stretched if you intend to play them on a widescreen TV.

You can also change the format of the video. The default is PAL (which is the TV standard for the UK).

Once you have set your options and added all your pictures and videos, click Next to display the Ready to burn disc screen, as shown in Figure 9-21.

Figure 9-21 Ready to burn the DVD

Depending on the options you chose, you will see the disc title and a menu on the screen, along with a background image.

You can also select from one of a number of different menu styles that are shown.

You can change both the font and the text for the menu by clicking on the Menu text button, which will bring up the screen shown in Figure 9-22.

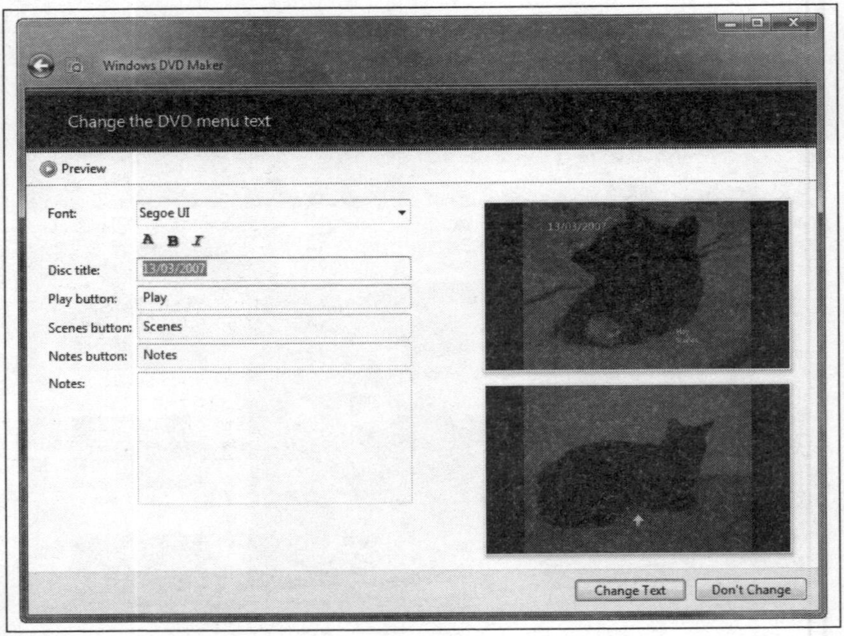

Figure 9-22 Changing the menu text

You can change the Disc title and also the text that appears on the menu buttons.

You can also customise the DVD menu by clicking on the Customise menu button, which will bring up the screen shown in Figure 9-23.

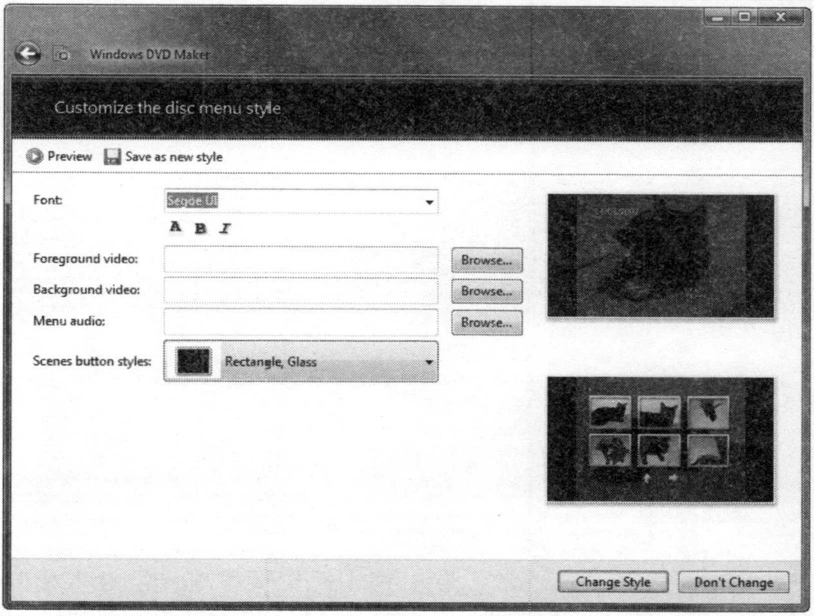

Figure 9-23 Customising the disc menu

From here you can change the style of the menu and add foreground and background video if you wish. You can also add some music to play during the menu playback.

If you want to change the settings for a slide show, click on the Slide Show button to launch the screen shown in Figure 9-24.

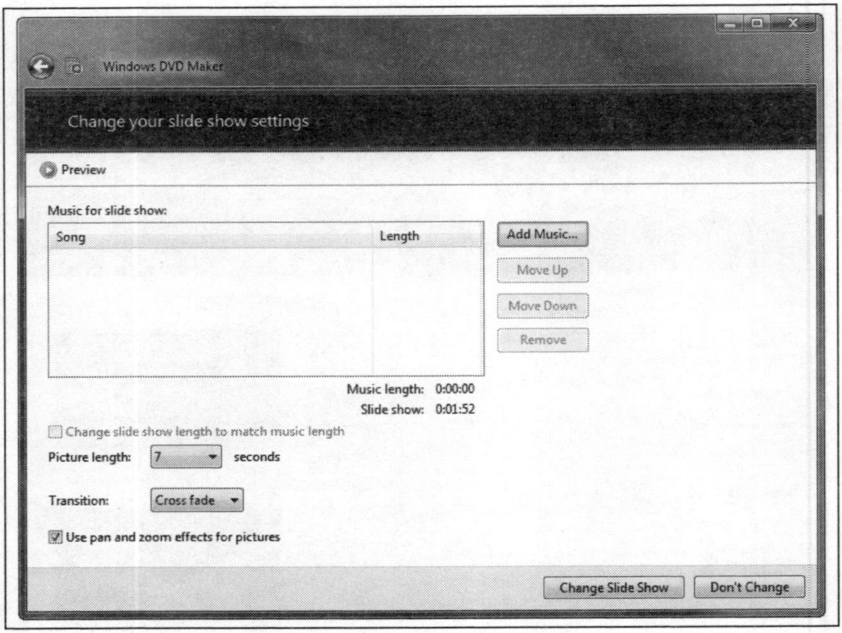

Figure 9-24 Changing slide show settings

From here you can add songs to be played during the slide show, change the sequence of the songs, change the length of time the pictures are displayed and also set the transitions to be used.

> A nice feature is the ability to change the length of the slide show to match the length of the music, so that your slide show does not end before the music has finished or the music finish before the end of the slide show.

When you have made all of the changes you want, click on the Burn button. You will be asked to insert a disc, as shown in Figure 9-25.

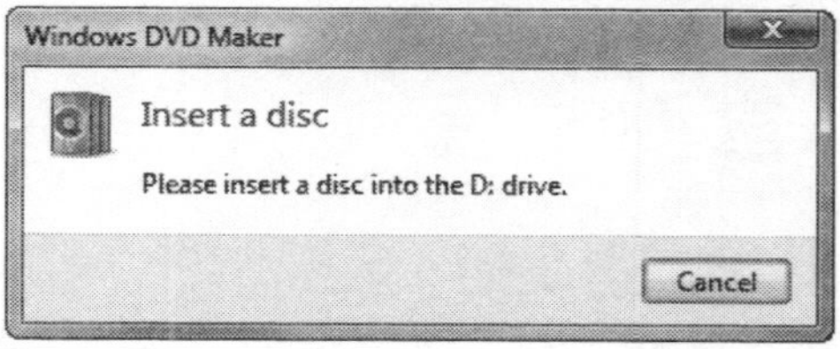

Figure 9-25 Prompted to insert a disc

Insert a blank disc and wait whilst the encoding and writing is performed. You will be able to monitor the progress of both the encoding and the writing, as shown in Figure 9-26.

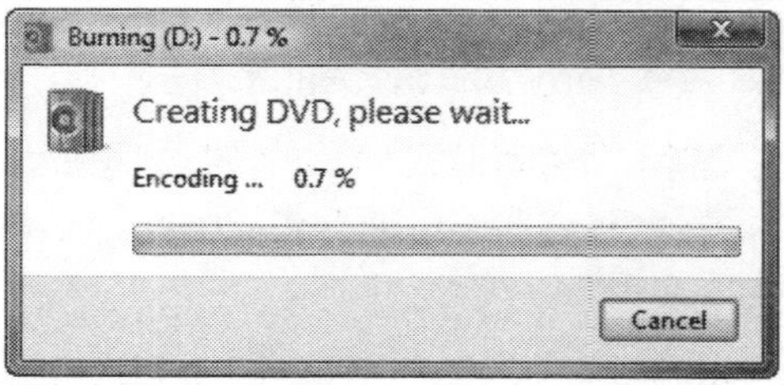

Figure 9-26 Monitoring the progress of the encoding and writing process

You need to be patient here – depending on the amount of music, pictures and videos you have added, the encoding and writing process may take some time.

When the process is complete, you will be informed that your disc is ready and you will have the option to make another copy of the disc, as shown in Figure 9-27.

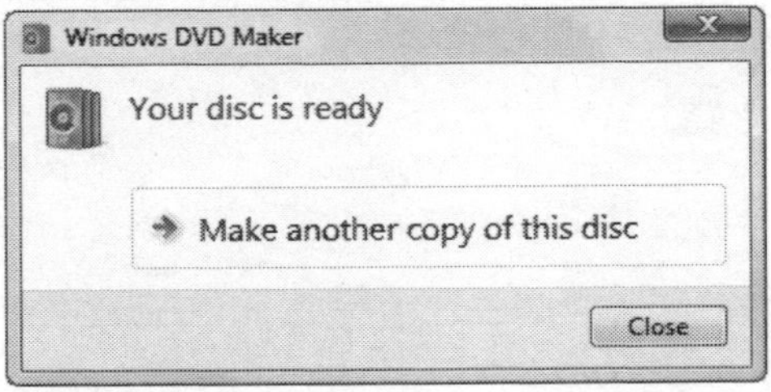

Figure 9-27 Do you want to make another copy?

If you are planning on giving copies of the disc to other people, now is a good time to create more copies. Of course you can always just copy the disc later.

Again, like the other programs mentioned in this chapter, the best way of finding out what they can do for you is to play around with them.

Summary

So now you have seen the programs that come with Windows Vista that can help you to easily manipulate and create DVDs, videos and more. Bear in mind that these programs have been designed to be as easy to use as possible and as such are not as feature-rich as some of the bigger commercial programs that are available.

10

Windows Media Center

For those of you who may be new to the concept of Windows Media Center, Microsoft has until the release of Windows Vista had a separate operating system version of Windows specifically for Media Center. The last version was Windows XP Media Center 2005 or MCE for short. You could not buy MCE in the shops or online, you had to buy an MCE machine, which came preinstalled with MCE. This was fine if you wanted to buy a new machine, but for those people who did not want to do that they were out of luck, that is until now.

Windows Media Center now comes preinstalled with Windows Vista Premium and Windows Vista Ultimate.

> If you want to use Windows Media Center then you will need to be running either Premium or Ultimate edition, it is not included in any other version of Windows.

This chapter will take a brief look at Windows Media Center, including some of the new functionality. It is not meant to be an in-depth guide to installing, configuring and using Media Center as that is a book all by itself. In fact, I have written a book on just this subject called "Windows Vista Media Center in easy steps" published by Computer Step and available at all good bookshops now.

What Does It Do?

Windows Media Center allows you to do a number of things, including:

- Watch and record your favourite TV shows and movies
- Listen to CDs, music and the radio
- Watch your DVDs
- View slideshows of your favourite pictures
- Choose what to watch from a 14-day TV guide
- Stream music and video to other rooms in your house using a Media Center Extender such as an Xbox 360

There are a number of improvements over the previous version of Media Center, including:

- A new and improved user interface with easier navigation (as can be seen in Figure 10-1)
- Media Center is now optimised for both widescreen and high definition (HD) displays

- A new Express setup option to enable you to jump straight into using Media Center and do the configurations later

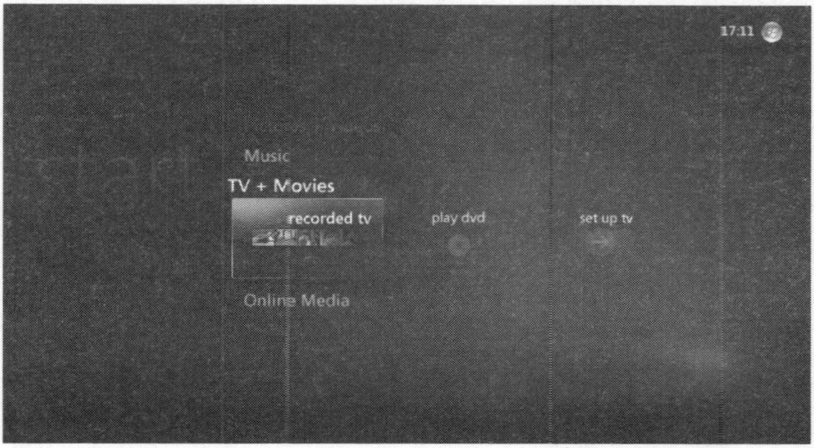

Figure 10-1 The New Windows Media Center User Interface

Requirements

Before you start to use Media Center you need to make sure that you have the correct hardware in order to use certain features – for example, if you are planning to watch TV through your Media Center you will need a TV Tuner Card installed.

> Make sure the TV Tuner Card you are planning to use supports Windows Vista.

You should also consider getting a Remote Control that is designed to control Media Center instead of using a keyboard and mouse. Media Center works perfectly well with a keyboard and mouse but if you truly want that full-blown Media Center experience, you should get a remote control so that you can control everything from the comfort of your sofa.

> If you have purchased a Windows Media Center computer then you should have all the correct hardware already installed and configured ready for you to use.

Setting Up Media Center

As mentioned earlier, Media Center comes preinstalled with Windows Premium and Ultimate editions, and so there is nothing extra to install. The only thing to do is actually perform the setup. To do this is quite simple; just launch Media Center for the first time and the setup wizard will start.

To launch Media Center you can either click on Windows Media Center after clicking the Start button or by selecting Windows Media Center from the Welcome Center screen and then clicking on Set up Windows Media Center, as shown in Figure 10-2. You may need to click the Show All Items…. link in order to display the Windows Media Center icon.

Figure 10-2 Starting Windows Media Center from the Welcome Center

You will be presented with the Welcome screen that can be seen in Figure 10-3. From here you can choose which setup option you want to use.

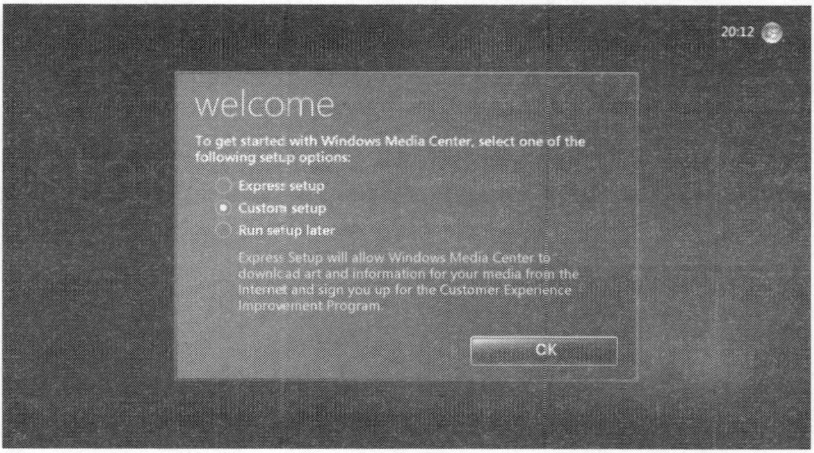

Figure 10-3 Windows Media Center Welcome Screen

The setup options are:

- Express setup – enables you to quickly get started with Media Center and automatically connects to the Internet to retrieve artwork on your behalf
- Custom setup – enables you to select different setup options yourself
- Run setup later – enables you to run setup at a later stage so that you can start using some of the functionality of Media Center without having to do anything

> The best option to choose is Custom Setup as you can specify all of your required settings; however, this setting can take a little time so make sure you have the time available before you select this option.

One of the other nice new features is the Automatic TV Signal Setup feature. What this does is automatically detect and configure any TV Tuner Cards that are installed and have sources such as an aerial, cable TV or Satellite TV connected to them, as shown in Figure 10-4. This saves you all of the hassle of having to configure the signals yourself. You can also choose whether to configure the TV signal based on the automatic detection or perform a manual setup.

From here you can also see if you have additional TV tuners installed but not configured. The example in Figure 10-4 shows that two TV cards were detected but only one could be automatically configured because the other did not have a TV signal, probably because it was not connected to anything.

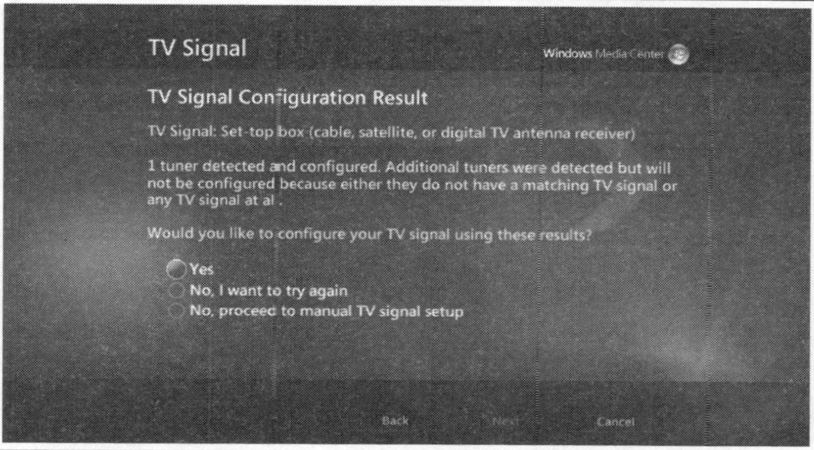

Figure 10-4 Results of the Automatic TV Signal Detection

If you want to use the Automatic TV Signal Setup feature, make sure you have connected a TV signal to each of the TV Tuner Cards you have installed before you start the setup process.

The Guide

The Guide is your 14-day electronic programme guide for all of the channels you have access to, as shown in Figure 10-5. This is configured automatically for you based on the selections you made for your TV signal during the setup process.

In order to keep the Guide up to date, make sure you have a connection to the Internet and either allow automatic updates to the Guide or perform periodic manual updates yourself.

Figure 10-5 The Guide

From the Guide you can click on a listing for more information and even choose to record a programme by selecting it. The red circle against Animal Park in Figure 10-5 indicates that it is currently being recorded.

You can scroll through the Guide and set a programme to record that is on at a later date as well. To make finding what you are looking for easier, you can choose to filter the Guide by categories and only display programme details for those categories. The categories include:

- Most viewed
- Film
- Sports
- Children
- News
- Special

You can also search by keywords such as an actor's name, a movie title or the title of the programme. Figure 10-6 shows the results of a Programme Title keyword search for Torchwood. You could then click on any of the results to see additional information displayed and make any selections you want, as shown in Figure 10-7.

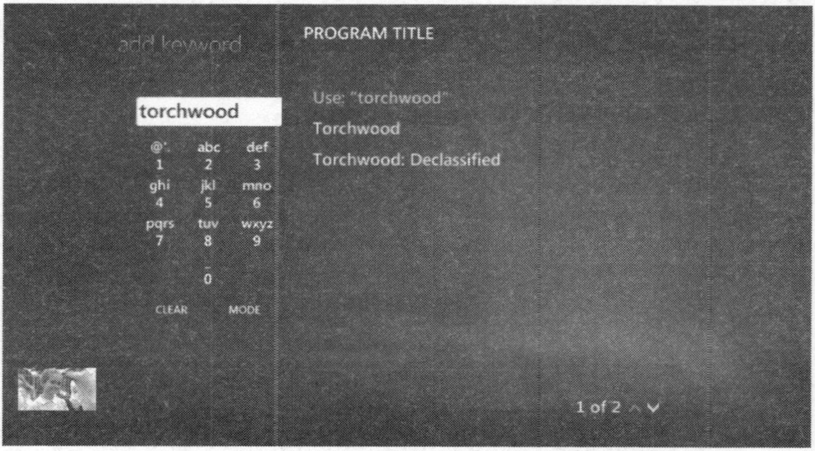

Figure 10-6 Searching for a Program Title

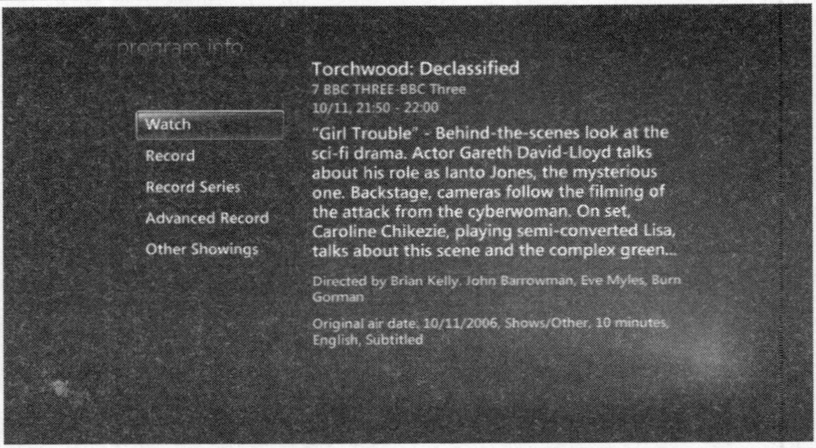

Figure 10-7 Additional Programme Information

TV and Movies

You can watch Live TV and Movies as they are being broadcast, or you can watch them later if you have recorded them.

You will only be able to watch Live TV if you have a properly configured TV Tuner Card installed.

You can change the channel using the remote control or mouse until you come to something you really want to watch.

Information about the programme (such as the name, channel and showing time) will then be displayed in a Mini-Guide window, as shown in Figure 10-8.

Figure 10-8 Watching Live TV

Watching DVDs

You can also use your Media Center to play back DVDs. All you need to do is place the DVD into the drive on the Media Center and sit back, watch and hopefully enjoy the movie.

If you have children, a really useful feature is the Parental Controls option. This enables you to set a maximum rating on the movies that are allowed to be watched; for example, only movies with a rating of 15 or less can be viewed, as shown in Figure 10-9. If a movie that is rated 18 is attempted to be played, Media Center will block it.

If you are going to use Parental Controls, it is a good idea to also Block Unrated Movies. This will block any movie that is unrated or whose rating cannot be confirmed.

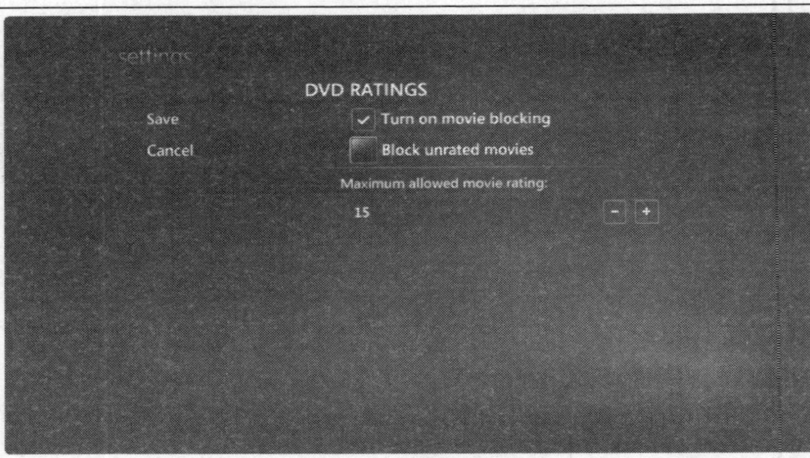

Figure 10-9 DVD Ratings for Parental Control

You have to set up a 4-digit pin to use Parental Controls, so make sure you don't use something that your children can easily guess, otherwise they can switch it off without your knowledge or consent.

Music and Radio

Media Center can be used as your one-stop music jukebox. You can play your favourite CD's, copying music to the Media Center, listen to the Radio and more.

If you want to listen to the Radio, you will need to have an FM Tuner card installed.

> Most TV Tuner Cards come with a built-in FM tuner as part of the card so check this before you buy a separate card.

When you play or copy music to your Media Center, if you have an Internet connection, Media Center will attempt to add album cover artwork and song information automatically for you to your Music Library. This is a very nice feature as it saves you having to manually enter all that information yourself. You can of course enter this information if Media Center cannot find it.

When you play a CD, you have the option to copy it to your Music Library by clicking the Copy CD button, as shown in Figure 10-10. As you can see, the Album title, artist, and track information has automatically been retrieved for you. All you need to do is click Copy CD and wait. Once the copying has been completed you can then just select the album or individual song from the Music Library. If you don't want to copy it to the Music Library you can just click on the Play Album button to listen to it instead.

Figure 10-10 Copying a CD to the Music Library

The Music Library contains all the songs, music and albums you have available on your Media Center. You can use different views, as shown in Figure 10-11, which is another great new feature, to help you decide what you want to listen to. For example, you can search by artist to display all the music by artist or you can even have the Program Library sort the songs by year, which can be fun if you want to listen to songs from a particular time.

You can also choose to write music CDs from your stored music if you want to.

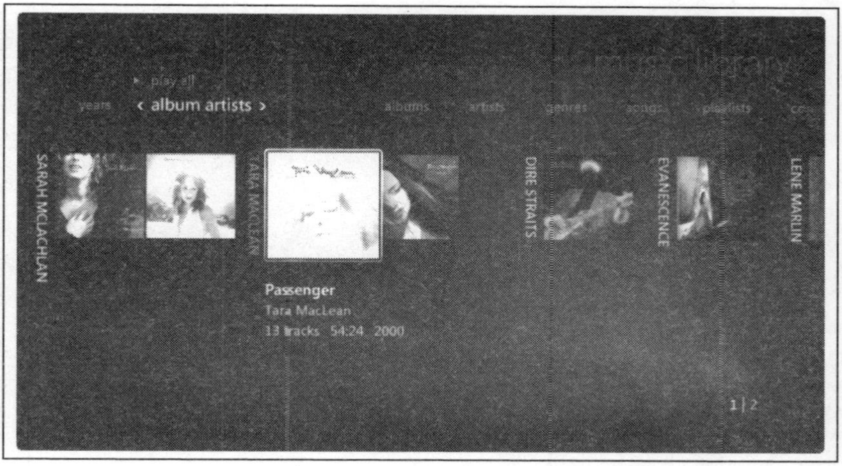

Figure 10-11 Artist View in the Music Library

Pictures and Videos

Media Center can also be used to store and display your pictures, videos and home movies. Once they are stored on your Media Center you can play slideshows of the pictures, manipulate and edit the pictures and even write CDs of your slideshows for others to view.

The Picture Library, as shown in Figure 10-12, contains all of your pictures. If you wanted to play a slideshow of those pictures, all you need to do is click the Play Slide Show button at the top of the screen.

> The Slide Show is optimised for High Definition displays so the pictures look great.

Figure 10-12 Pictures in the Picture Library

You can then rotate the picture, or touch it up, which includes the ability to crop the picture and adjust the contrast and the red-eye settings. You can also print your pictures from here.

> If you want to perform any serious image manipulation you should do so outside of Windows Media Center as the functionality is very limited.

Writing CDs and DVDs

Media Center includes the functionality to write different types of CDs and DVDs, including music and slideshows, data discs and also the option to create DVDs of your recorded TV programmes so that they can be played back on a normal DVD player later on, as shown in Figure 10-13.

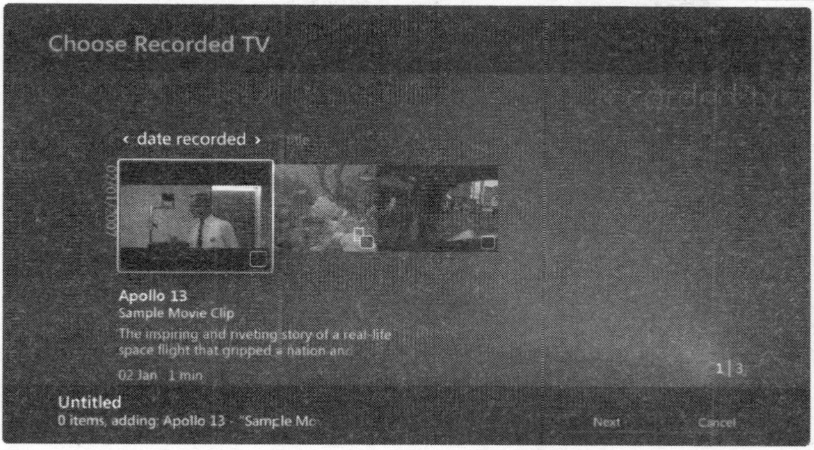

Figure 10-13 Writing a DVD of Recorded TV

> The formats you can write to will depend on the type of hardware you have installed.

Media Center Extenders

If you want to watch or listen to content stored on your Media Center in a different room in your house from the one that the Media Center is located in, you can do so using a Media Center Extender.

A Media Center Extender is a piece of hardware that can be located in any room in the house and then connects over your network (either via a wired or a wireless connection) back to your Media Center computer and then streams the chosen content.

> Even though the Media Extender works using a wireless connection, it is advisable, where possible, to use a wired connection to reduce any playback issues you may experience.

Currently, the only supported Extender is the Microsoft Xbox 360 console, as shown in Figure 10-14.

Figure 10-14 A Microsoft Xbox 360 Console

For more information on configuring your Xbox 360 as a Windows Media Center Extender, and also seeing what else you can do with an Xbox 360 other than playing games, take a look at my book "Getting More From Your Microsoft Xbox 360" which is also published by Babani Books and is available from all good book sellers.

Online Media

Those of you who have used the previous version of Media Center may remember the Online Spotlight. To be honest, most people found it lacked any real reason to use it, as better content could be found just by surfing the Internet from the Media Center computer. Online Spotlight has been replaced with Online Media which enables your Media Center computer to receive special online content, as shown in Figure 10-15.

Figure 10-15 Online Media Showcase

You can easy search for content that has been sorted into different views, including:

- TV + Movies
- Music + Radio
- News + Sports
- Games
- And more

As time goes on, this content will increase. Keep checking back to see if there is anything that interests you.

Summary

I hope that you will now have a better understanding of what Windows Media Center can do and how you can use to enhance your media experience. There really is a lot more to Media Center than has been covered in this chapter, I have barely scratched the surface. Have a play with Media Center, see what else it can do, decide for yourself if it is something, you want to use. Chances are you will be hooked after a short while, most people are.

11

Security

Security is a big concern for most people – it really should be a big concern for everyone! There are more security threats out there today than ever before, but it's not all doom and gloom. Windows Vista contains a number of applications and built-in functionality to combat some of these threats. Now it is very important to note that the features in Windows Vista should be used in conjunction with other applications, such as anti-virus, and also some of the applications, such as Windows Defender need to be continually updated to maintain the protection levels you really need.

This chapter will be looking at some of these applications, including User Account Control, Windows Defender and Parental Controls.

User Account Control

A lot of people use an "administrator" account when using Windows. This is usually because the default account that is created has administrator privileges. Obviously if you are logged in with those sorts of privileges then should your computer be compromised in any way, pretty much anything could be done either without your knowledge or certainly without your consent. This is where user account control comes into play. Basically, any time an application or process attempts to do something that could affect the running of your computer, user access control kicks in and asks you to verify that you are happy for that process to continue, and sometimes even enter your password again to confirm. At first this may seem like a real pain, I for one started turning it off, but I soon realised that there were not that many occasions when I legitimately wanted to do something that would warrant user access control intervening, so I switched it back on!

Should you decide to switch it off, or even switch it back on, you can easily do so by selecting User Accounts and Family Safety from Control Panel, then selecting User Accounts and choosing which account you want to change and finally clicking on Turn User Account Control on or off.

All you then need to do is remove or add a tick in the box, as shown in Figure 11-1.

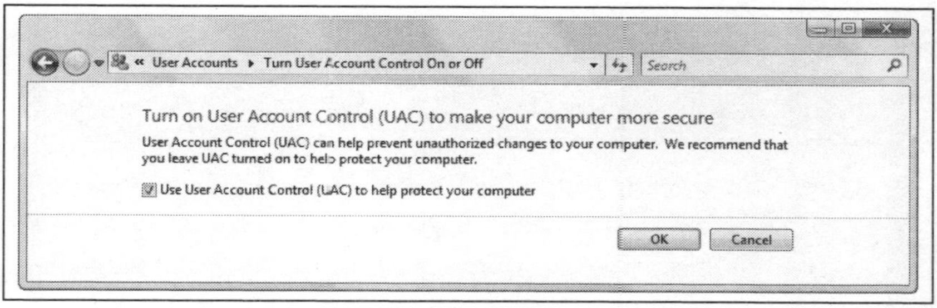

Figure 11-1 User Account Control

Windows Defender

Windows Defender is Microsoft's answer to anti-spyware. It scans your computer for any spyware or unwanted applications and also provides real-time protection for key system locations.

Windows Defender can be launched from the Start Menu and when it starts displays a screen similar to the one shown in Figure 11-2.

You can choose to run a scan at any time by clicking the Scan button. This will perform what is known as a Quick Scan which examines key files and areas. If you want to manually check all of your files then choose Full Scan by clicking on the down arrow next to the Scan button.

Scans can often take quite a while to complete – especially if you have selected a Full Scan, so be patient.

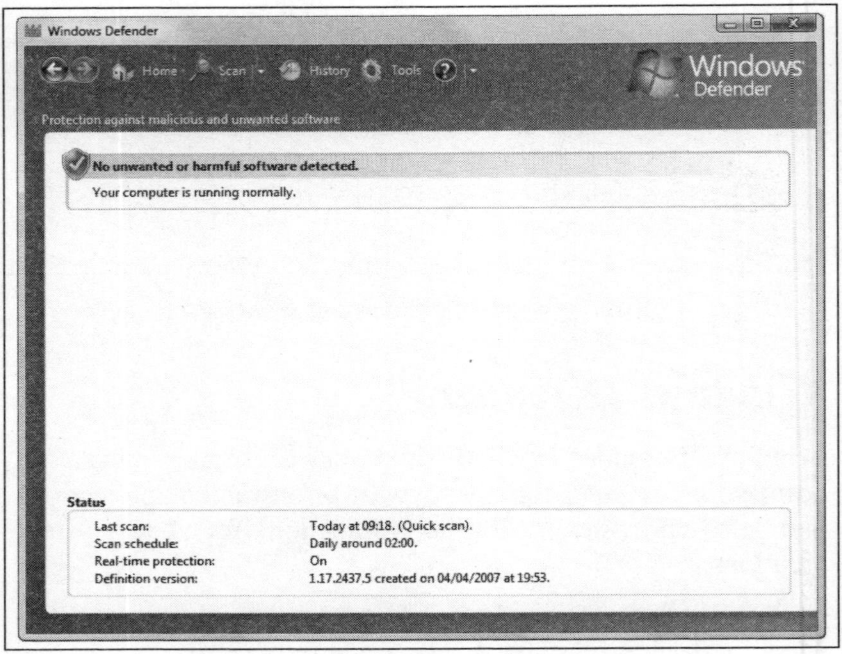

Figure 11-2 Windows Defender

Windows Defender is automatically updated as part of the normal Windows Update procedure – so if you have not set your updates to automatic you must make sure that you perform regular manual updates, to ensure that Windows Defender is updated and has all the latest information about threats that might affect your computer.

You can change the default options in Windows Defender, such as when a scan is performed, by clicking on the Tools button and choosing options. This will display the screen shown in Figure 11-3.

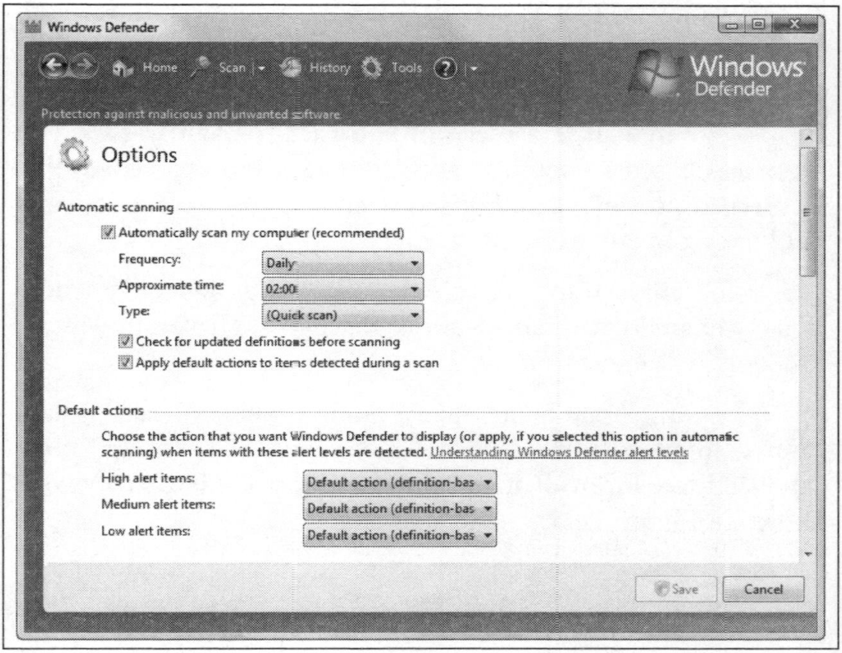

Figure 11-3 Changing the options for Windows Defender

You can then make any changes you need, remembering to click on the Save button.

Unless you are using some other form of anti-spyware software you should not switch off Windows Defender!

The Windows Firewall

Windows Vista, like Windows XP SP2 before it, comes with its own built-in Firewall, known strangely enough as the Windows Firewall.

A Firewall is a piece of software (or hardware if you have purchased something more elaborate and expensive) that is used to prevent unauthorised access to your computer and network from any external source.

Usually, Firewalls block everything and only allow what you instruct them to allow through. These allowances are known as exceptions.

To find out about the Windows Firewall settings on your computer, from Control Panel select Security and click on Windows Firewall to display a screen similar to the one shown in Figure 11-4.

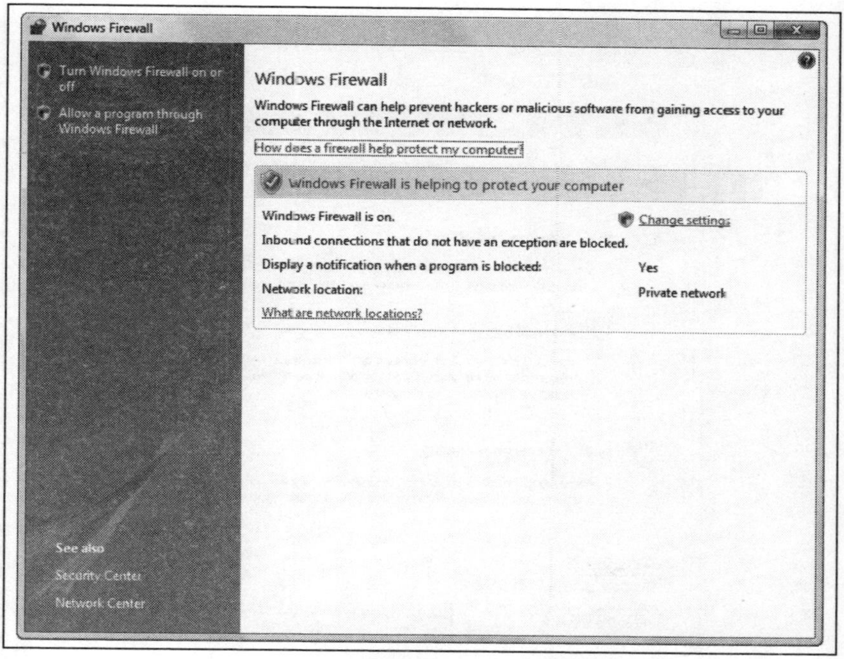

Figure 11-4 The Windows Firewall

From here you can see if the Windows Firewall is switched on and other useful information. If you need to change the settings for any reason, click on Change settings which will display the Windows Firewall settings screen, as shown in Figure 11-5.

> You should not switch off the Windows Firewall if you do not have any other firewall running.

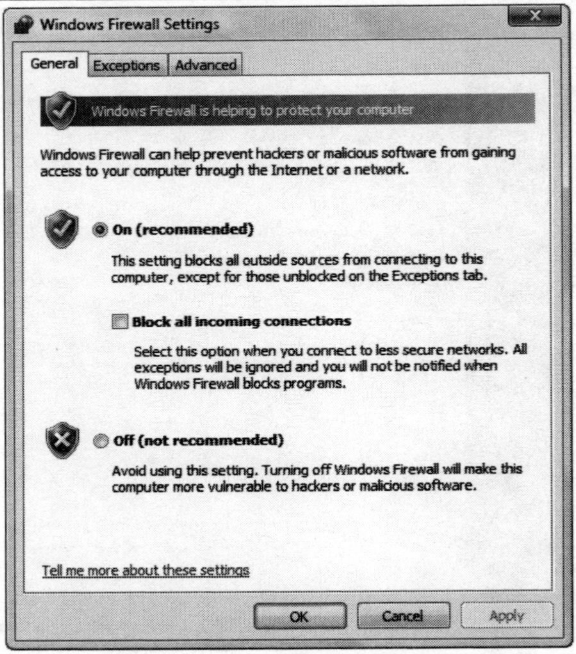

Figure 11-5 Windows Firewall Settings

If you click on the Exceptions tab, any exceptions that have been added either manually, or by Windows on your behalf, are displayed, as shown in Figure 11-6.

Here you can add a program or a port, edit an existing exception or even delete one.

Be very careful if you want to add an exception yourself – make sure you have all the information you need from a reputable source.

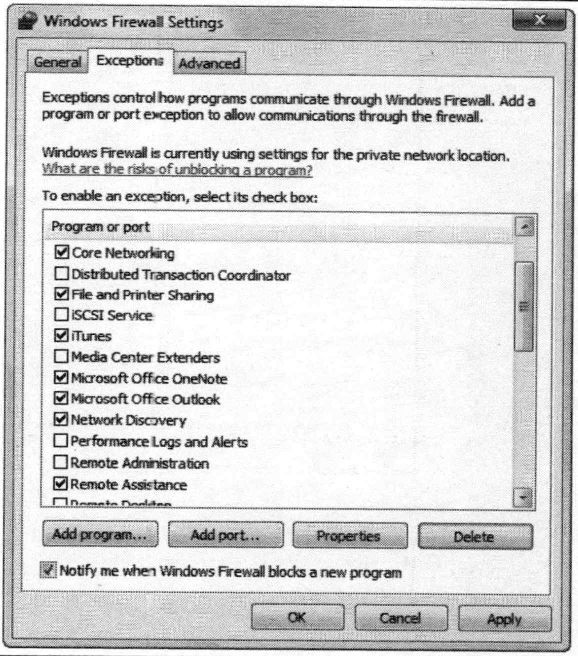

Figure 11-6 Windows Firewall Exceptions

Security Center

The Security Center is the place to go for all-round information on your security settings. From here you can easily see if you have any security concerns, if applications providing security functionality are working, and more.

You can start the Security Center by selecting Security and then Security Center from Control Panel. Figure 11-7 shows the Security Center in operation.

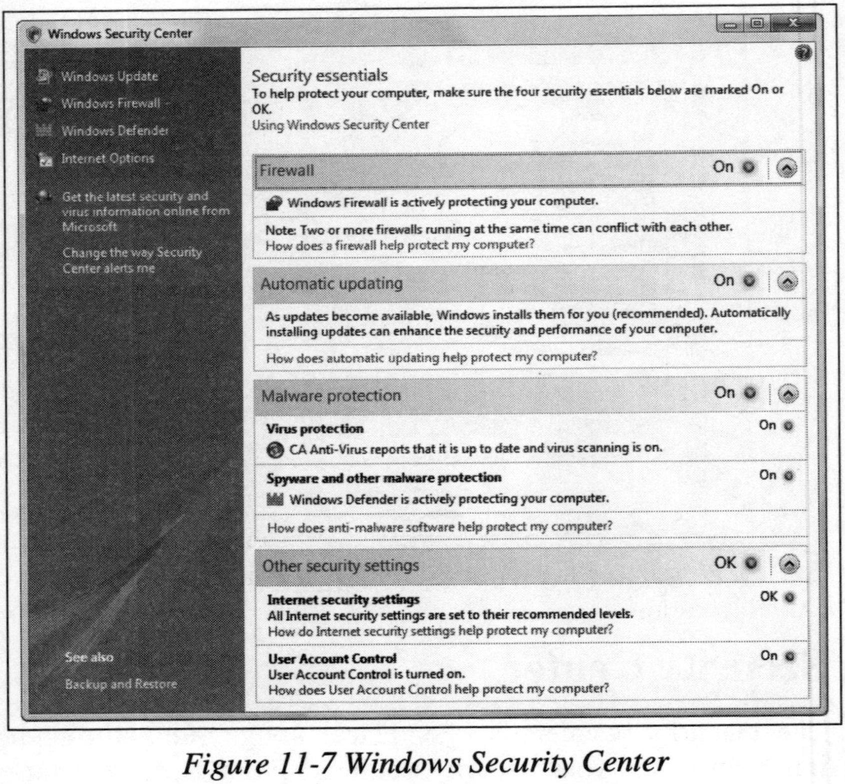

Figure 11-7 Windows Security Center

As you can see from Figure 11-7, all of my security applications are functioning correctly. If they weren't, you will see warnings, in which case you need to address them immediately.

Parental Controls

Whilst strictly speaking Parental Controls are not exactly used to enforce security they do provide a level of protection if you have children. This protection includes:

- Being able to limit when and for how long your children can use the computer
- Control which websites your children can view
- Restrict access to games, based on the title, content or rating of the game
- See detailed reports about usage

To launch the Parental Controls panel, as shown in Figure 11-8 go to Control Panel and select Security, then click on Parental Controls and choose the account you want to apply controls to.

By default the Parental Controls are switched off, so the first thing you will need to do is click the On, enforce current settings button.

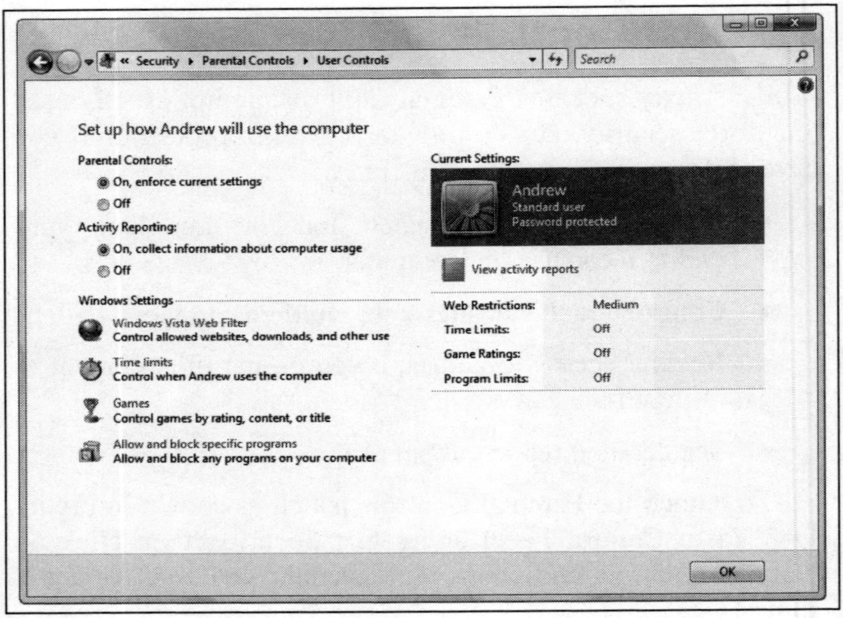

Figure 11-8 Parental Controls Panel

Then click each of the Windows Settings link in turn and make any selections, as in Figure 11-9 which controls the Time Limits.

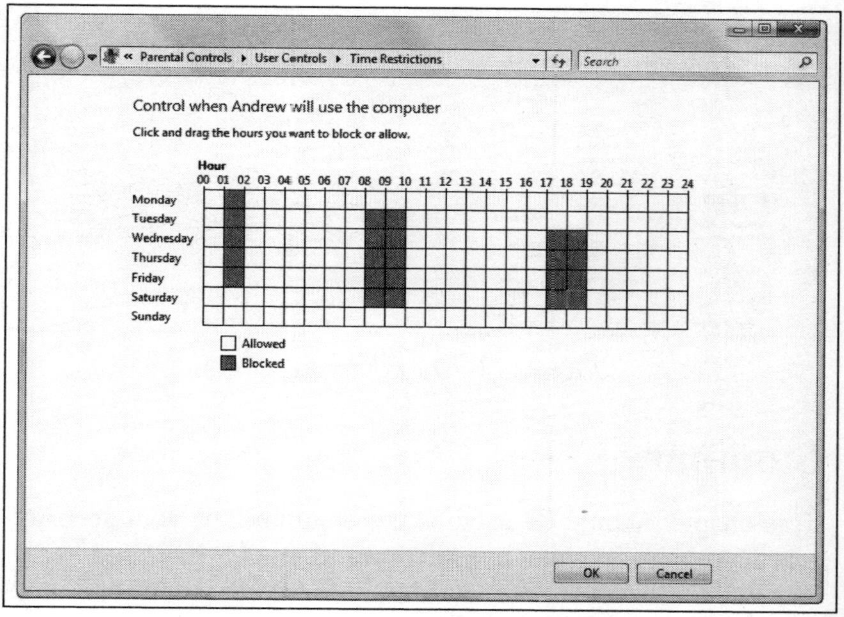

Figure 11-9 Enforcing Time Limits

At any time you can then view detailed reports by simply clicking on the View activity reports link. An example report is shown in Figure 11-10.

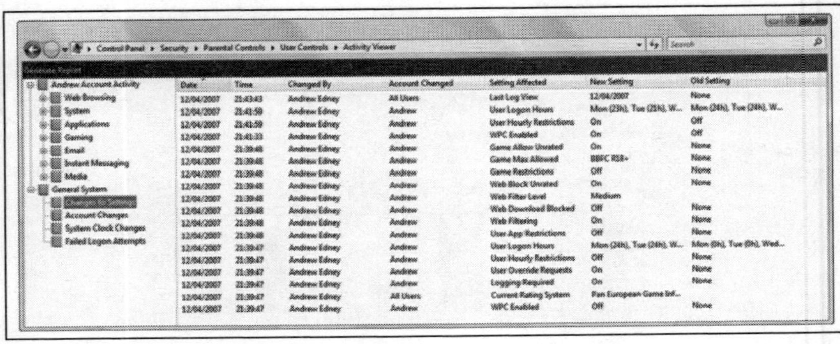

Figure 11-10 Activity Report

Summary

This chapter should be used as the beginning of your security journey. New threats are discovered every day and it is imperative that you are constantly on guard and that any applications that you are using are updated on a regular basis. Whatever happens, do not take security for granted.

12

Troubleshooting

As this is the last chapter, I thought it might be useful to include a few troubleshooting steps that could help you resolve some issues you might experience. This is by no means an exhaustive list, that would take another book itself!

Memory Issues

A fairly common problem, certainly one I have experienced a few times, is caused by faulty memory. Windows Vista uses a process called ASLR – Address Space Layout Randomisation. This process will use random portions of RAM for additional security to stop hackers from possible exploits, however this does mean that as Vista tries to use a portion of RAM that might be bad, then it will crash – usually with a nice blue screen!

Windows XP always used a set portion of the RAM and so may never have accessed a bad part which is why you may have used that RAM without a problem.

Windows Vista comes with a memory diagnostics tool to help you determine if the memory you are using is faulty. If it is, you should contact the supplier of the memory for a replacement if it is still in warranty.

To run the Vista Memory Diagnostics Tool, follow these steps:

1. Click the Start button.
2. In the search box, type memory.
3. This should display the Memory Diagnostics Tool link, as shown in Figure 12-1. Click it to start.

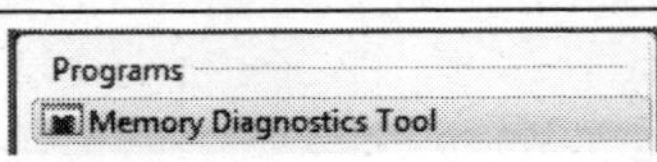

Figure 12-1 Starting the Memory Diagnostics Tool

4. You will then need to decide when to check for the potential memory problems, as shown in Figure 12-2. You can either have Vista restart now and check or you can choose to check next time you restart Vista yourself.

If you are having memory problems you really should choose to restart and check immediately before you lose anything important in a crash.

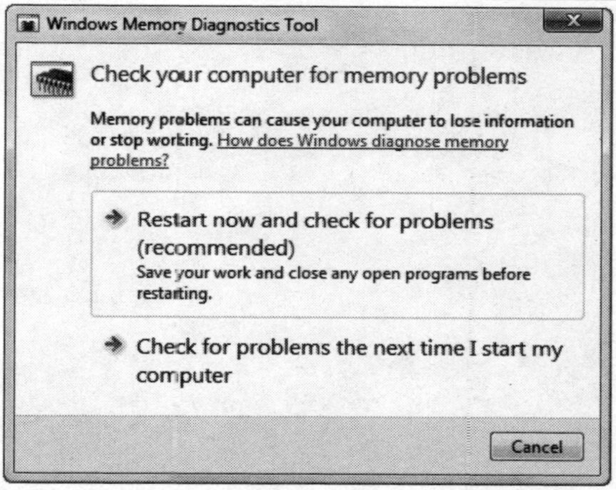

Figure 12-2 Choosing when to check for memory problems

5. When Windows restarts, the Windows Memory Diagnostics Tool will start automatically, as shown in Figure 12-3. The default scan will perform a standard test mix and perform the actual scan twice. Once the scan is completed Windows will restart the computer automatically and display the test results for you.

It is advisable to change the scan test mix type from standard to extended so that more in-depth tests are performed. Note however that these tests will take considerably longer to perform but the results will be more thorough.

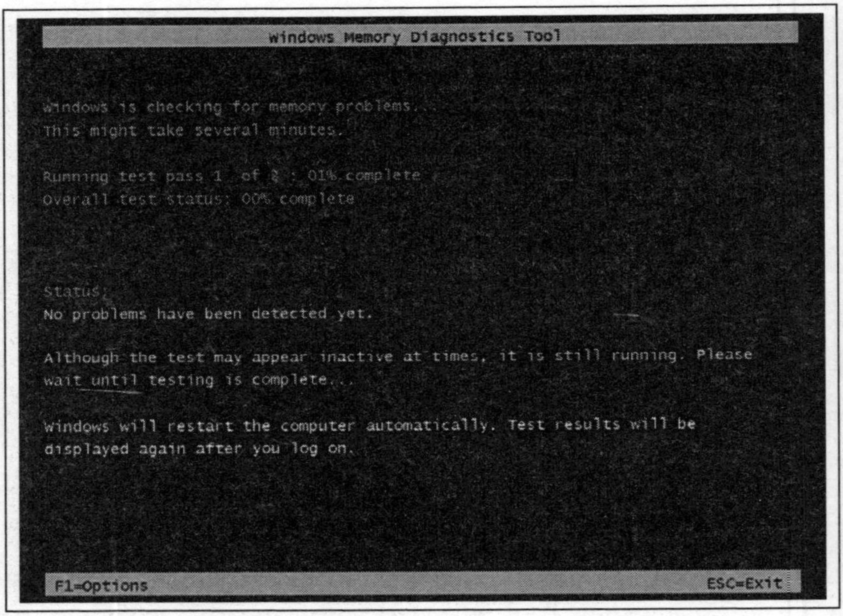

Figure 12-3 The Windows Memory Diagnostics Tool

6. Press F1 to open the Options screen, as shown in Figure 12-4.
7. Use the down arrow on your keyboard to change the test from Standard to Extended.
8. If you want to change the Cache test or the test pass count, use the TAB key to move to them.
9. Press F10 to apply the changes and run the tests.

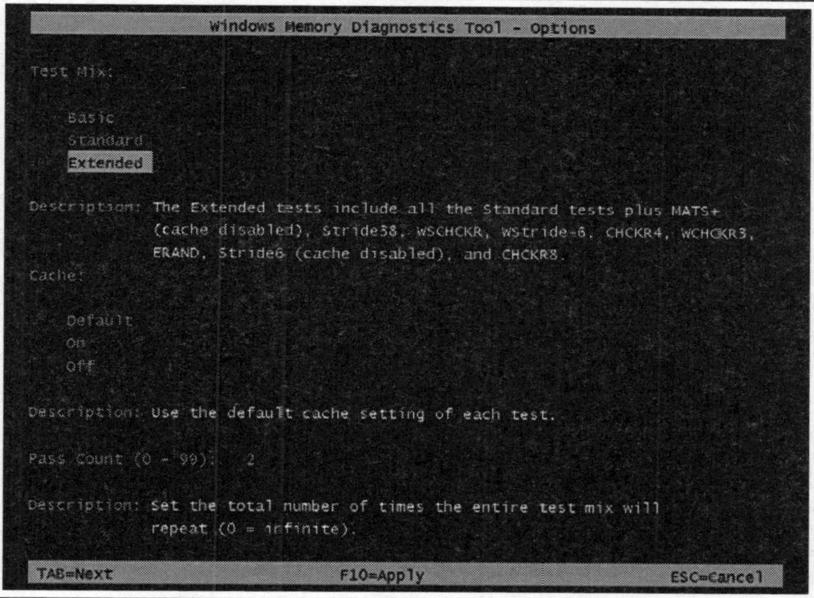

Figure 12-4 Diagnostic Tool Options screen

Internet Connection Problems

If you are experiencing problem with your Internet Connection, you can have Windows perform some Network Diagnostics on your behalf.

1. Open the Network and Sharing Center, as shown in Figure 12-5.

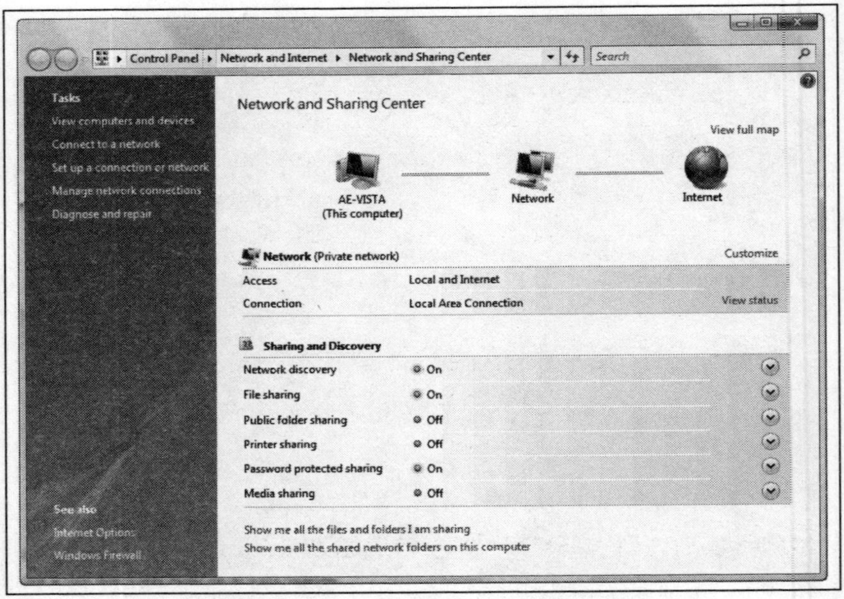

Figure 12-5 The Network and Sharing Center

2. Click on Diagnose and repair from the Tasks list.
3. Windows will then perform a scan, as shown in Figure 12-6.

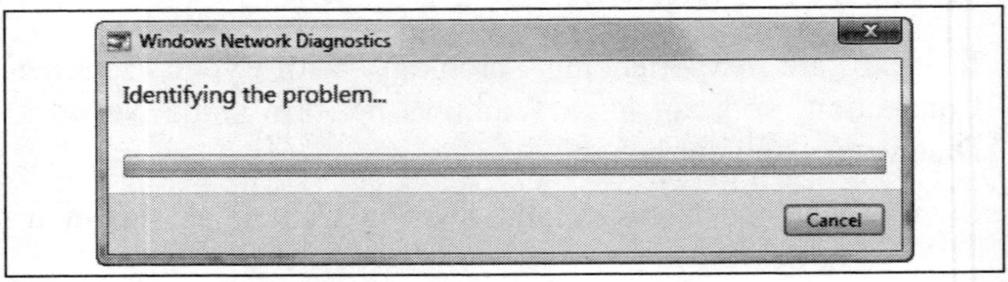

Figure 12-6 Performing a scan

4. The results of the scan are then displayed, as shown in Figure 12-7. If problems are diagnosed, follow the additional steps that are displayed.

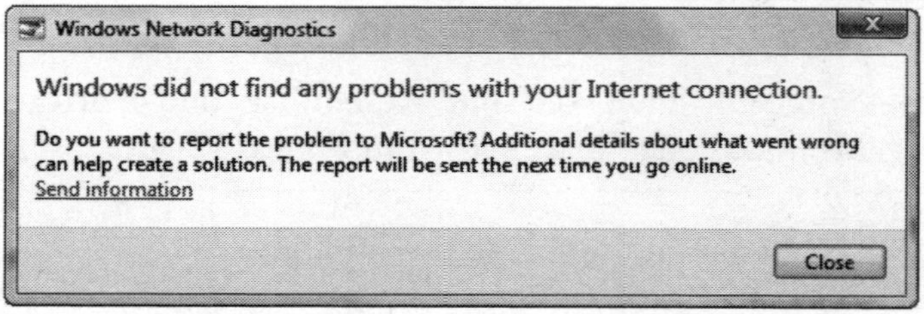

Figure 12-7 Results of the scan

Reliability and Performance Monitor

You can have Windows run system diagnostics for you and display the results along with other useful information. This can be very useful in troubleshooting a variety of different problems, including disc space issues and security problems.

1. Click the Start button.
2. In the search box, type reliability.
3. This should display the Reliability and System Performance Monitor link, as shown in Figure 12-8. Click it to start.

Figure 12-8 Starting the Reliability and Performance Monitor tool

4. You will then see the Reliability and Performance Monitor console, as shown in Figure 12-9.

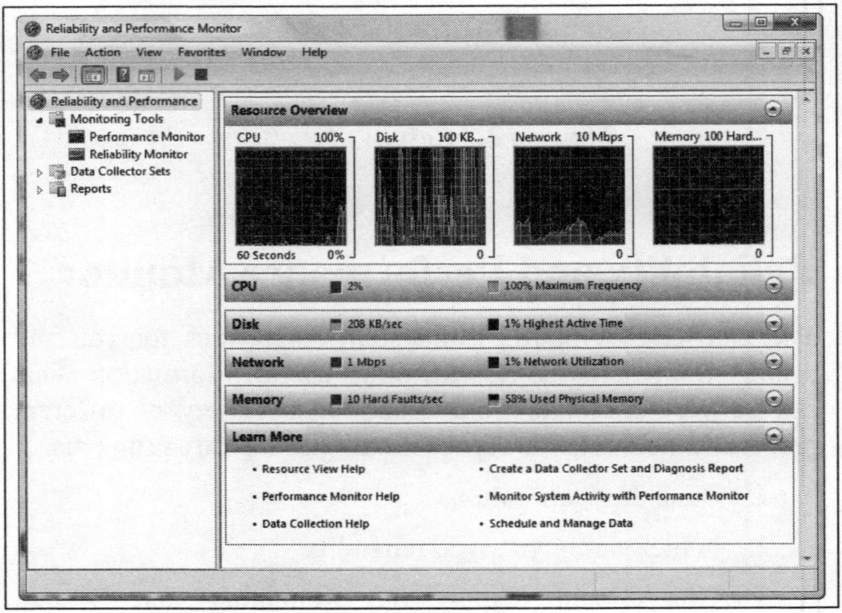

Figure 12-9 The Reliability and Performance Monitor console

There is a lot of information available from the console so take a look at the different elements and get to know what each is for.

5. If you produce a System Diagnostics Report, you can view it by Clicking on Reports, System, System Diagnostics and selecting the date of the report. This will display that report, as shown in Figure 12-10.

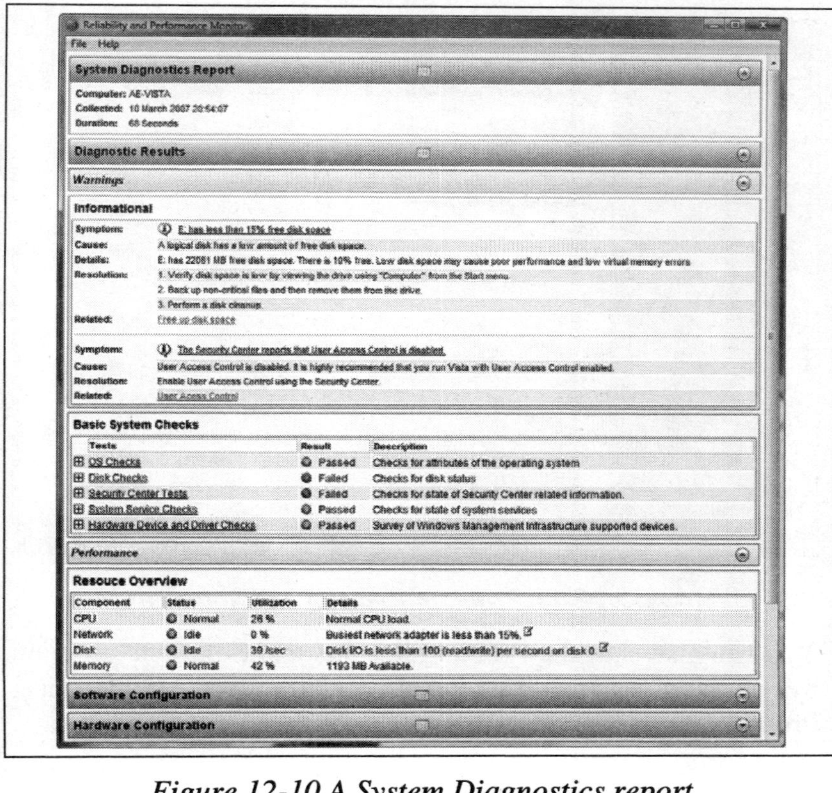

Figure 12-10 A System Diagnostics report

Problem Reports and Solutions

Windows will occasionally report problems to you and attempt to give you solutions. Figure 12-11 shows a problem report with some solutions. To view a solution or a report, just click on it.

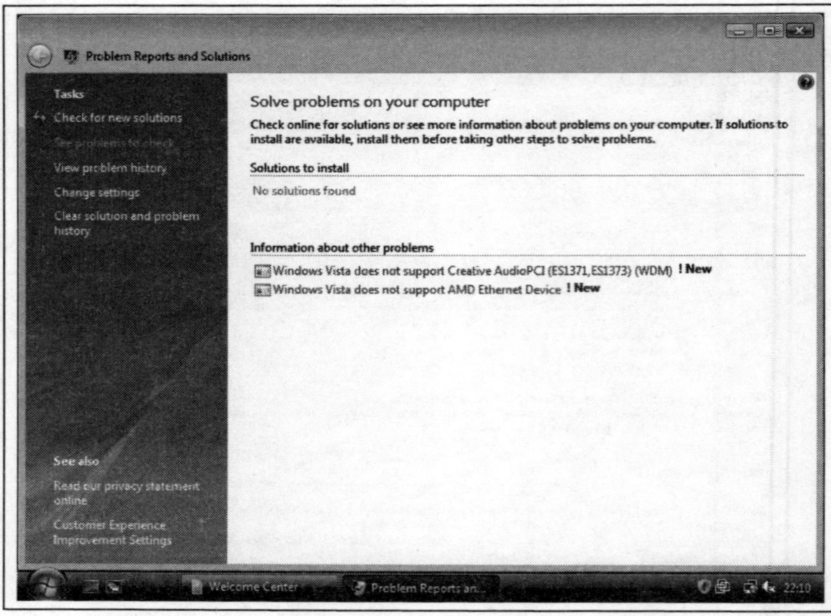

Figure 12-11 Problem Reports and Solutions

You can also start the Problem Reports and Solutions program by clicking on Control Panel, System and Maintenance, Problem Reports and Solutions.

You can then click on Check for new solutions from the Tasks list to send information to Microsoft and see if any new solutions are available.

> If you have any outstanding problems, it is worth checking on a regular basis to see if they have a resolution yet.

Summary

Hopefully these few insights into how to troubleshoot issues will have been helpful. Don't forget that a great source of troubleshooting advice is available on the Internet – just search for your problem and you should find some help or even the answer you are looking for. Just try and be as specific as you can in your search to narrow it down a little.

Index

32-bit 4

64-bit 4

Activating Windows Vista 62

Activity Reports 215

Adding Pictures 164

Aero 75

Aero Glass 75

Base Score 82

Burning Music CDs 148

Clean Install 48

ClearType 78

Command Bar 73

Control Panel 91

Cropping Pictures 167

Customising Network Settings 114

Details Pane 74

Device Manager 61

Dialog Boxes 79

Drive Partitions 53

Explorer 73

Favourites 124

Firewall Exceptions 208

Fixing Pictures 167

Fixing Red Eye 168

Flip 76

Flip 3D 77

Gadgets 84

Gadget Gallery 85

Hardware Requirements 15

High Definition 153, 184

Installation Selection 52

Instant Search 73

Internet Explorer 7 117

Live Icons 73

Media Center Extenders 199

Media Guide 151

Media Player 11 135

Media Player Library 141

Memory Diagnostics Tool 218

Memory Issues 217

Mini Player 151

Music and Radio 195

Navigation Pane 73

Network and Sharing Center 112

Network Map 113

Networking

Networking 107

Passphase 110

Wired 107

Wireless 108

Online Media 201

Online Printing 168

Parental Controls 213-216

Performing the Upgrade 42

Phishing Filter 128

Pictures and Videos 197

Playlists 147

Pop-up Blocker 126

Post Installation Tasks 60

Preview Pane 74

Printing Pictures 170

Privacy Options 136

Problem Reports 226

Product Key 51

Protected Content Migration 33-41

Protected Mode 131

Reliability and Performance Monitor 223

Ripping Music 143

Rip Options 145

RSS Feeds 132

Searching the Internet 118

Security 203

Security Center 211

Setting Date and Time 58

Slide Shows 171

Start Menu 71

Subscore 84

Sync 150

Tabs

Quick Tabs 122

Tabbed Browsing 120

The Guide 189

Troubleshooting 217

TV and Movies 192

Upgrading 19

User Account Control 204

Vista Capable 18

Vista Premium Ready 18

Welcome Center 89-91

Windows Anytime Upgrade 65

Windows Backup and Restore 93-105

Windows Defender 205

Windows Display Driver Model 75

Windows DVD Maker 172

Windows Easy Transfer 21-33

Windows Experience Index 81

Windows Firewall 208

Windows Genuine Advantage 64

Windows Media Center 7, 18, 182

Windows Movie Maker 153

Windows Photo Gallery 163

Windows Sidebar 84

Windows Tablet 18

Windows Vista Editions

Windows Vista Business 8, 16

Windows Vista Enterprise 9, 16

Windows Vista Home Basic 5, 17

Windows Vista Home Premium 6, 16

Windows Vista Starter 10, 17

Windows Vista Ultimate 7, 16

Windows Vista Upgrade Advisor 33

Windows XP Media Center Edition 4

Windows XP Tablet Edition 4

Wizards 79

Writing CDs and DVDs 198

Xbox 360 200

Notes

Take a note of the configuration details for your equipment for future reference:

System serial number:

Windows Vista serial number:

Windows Vista version:

Product activation date:

Network name:

Wireless configuration details:

IP address:

Subnet mark:

Default gateway:

DNS addresses (if applicable):

Printer details:

Any other information: